The Heart of Unconditional Love

THE HEART OF UNCONDITIONAL LOVE

A Powerful New Approach to Loving-Kindness Meditation

TULKU THONDUP

EDITED BY
Harold Talbott *and* Lydia Segal

SHAMBHALA
Boston & London
2015

SHAMBHALA PUBLICATIONS, INC.
Horticultural Hall
300 Massachusetts Avenue
Boston, Massachusetts 02115
www.shambhala.com

© 2015 by Tulku Thondup Rinpoche

The Buddhayana Foundation Series XIII

Line art on p. iii by Robert Beer, used with permission.
Photograph of Shadakshari Avalokiteshvara opposite p. 112
reproduced courtesy of Sotheby's, Inc. © 2005.
Standing Avalokiteshvara opposite p. 113 by Zashi Nima,
used with permission.

9 8 7 6 5 4 3 2 1

FIRST EDITION
Printed in the United States of America

♾ This edition is printed on acid-free paper that meets the
American National Standards Institute z39.48 Standard.
♻ This book is printed on 30% postconsumer recycled paper.
For more information please visit www.shambhala.com.

Distributed in the United States by Penguin Random House LLC
and in Canada by Random House of Canada Ltd

Designed by Lora Zorian

LIBRARY OF CONGRESS CATALOGING-IN-PUBLICATION DATA

Thondup, Tulku, author.
The heart of unconditional love: a powerful new approach to
loving-kindness meditation / Tulku Thondup.
pages   cm
978-1-61180-235-1 (paperback)
1. Meditation—Buddhism. 2. Compassion—
Religious aspects—Buddhism. I. Title.
BQ5612.T49 2015
294.3´4435—dc23
2014020623

In memory of Elsie P. Mitchell

Contents

PREFACE

This book differs in significant ways from my earlier book, *The Healing Power of Loving-Kindness* (2009). That work emphasizes the development of loving-kindness in the traditional way, which focuses first on individuals such as a loved one (for example, one's mother) and then on others. The uniqueness of the present book is that it offers new ways of applying loving-kindness meditation, as well as new and more effective ways of perfecting the highest states of loving-kindness, unconditional love.

In this book, we try from the very beginning to generate unconditional love in ourselves by feeling the Buddha's unconditional love through devotion and to serve others with that love. We try to see the whole world as a world of unconditional love and to perfect the ultimate unconditional love that is free from concepts. I have not explicitly written about this anywhere else, nor seen it in other books. This is the first time I have talked about transforming oneself and the world through this meditation. Yet, at the same time, this presentation extracts the very heart essence of Buddhism's ageless wisdom teachings.

The transformation is anchored in the fact that when our mind is immersed in loving-kindness, it becomes a mind of loving-kindness, and all our perceptions and actions reflect that. This premise is so simple, so understandable, and so logical. It is a new way of presenting, thinking about, and conceiving of ourselves and the world as the heart of the Buddha's loving-kindness and of finding the Buddha within. The origin of the book and how I came to discover the method of loving-kindness meditation according to "Four Buddha Stages" are explained in the Introduction.

There is quite a bit of repetition in the book. Whenever I get the chance, I explain things over and over. That's because, by repeatedly focusing on the words, meanings, and experiences of loving-kindness, we can better extract its essence, like honeybees accumulating an abundance of nectar by extracting it repeatedly from the flowers. This principle applies in many areas: devotees receive blessings by praying repeatedly; laundry is cleaned by repeated washing cycles; dough is made soft and pliable by repeated kneading; and muscles are made stronger by many "reps" of exercise. Also, with repetition, terms and ideas that are initially strange for many of us—including the meaning and the experience of unconditional love—become understandable, then familiar, then enjoyable—and finally, our own intimate nature.

With the aim of making this book more accessible to readers who are somewhat new to Buddhism, I have added a glossary of terms that might be unfamiliar to some. The endnotes are reserved primarily for scholarly citations and linguistic information. For the sake of brevity, abbreviations keyed to the Bibliography have been used in endnotes for Tibetan-language text titles. (Please see the paragraph introducing the notes, on page 217, for more details.)

I hope it will become clear that you don't have to be a so-called Buddhist to meditate on and pray to the Buddha of Loving-Kindness. If you belong to another tradition and prefer, you can adapt the methods in this book to pray to and meditate on the source of loving-kindness of your own tradition. The important point is that the source of blessings should be the embodiment of unconditional love for all beings.

ACKNOWLEDGMENTS

I am grateful to Harold Talbott for lending his gifted knowlege and unstinting dedication in editing this book thoroughly, as he has kindly been doing for my writings for over three decades. I am grateful to Lydia Segal, my wife, for carefully editing this book with her literary gifts. Our deeply shared devotion in the beauty of loving-kindness inspired me to offer this book, which is as much her book as mine.

I am greatly indebted to Michael Baldwin for single-handedly providing all the facilities I could possibly want for my research and writing projects. I am thankful to the members and the patrons of The Buddhayana Foundation for most generously supporting my research and writing for the past thirty-three years. I will always be grateful to Fred Segal and Micheline Segal for their kindness and care. I offer my gratitude to my Dharma teachers, loving parents, noble grandparents, and the kind friends who shared their unconditional love in every possible way.

I am deeply thankful to Nikko Odiseos and Samuel Bercholz for providing the perfect channel for the wisdom of unconditional love to reach readers. I am especially indebted to Kendra Crossen Burroughs for refining the book with her true editorial mastery and dedication. I am thankful to Hazel Bercholz and Lora Zorian for their beautiful design work, and to Jonathan Green, Liz Shaw, John Golebiewski, and other staff members at Shambhala Publications for bringing this book into final form with indispensable care. Appreciation is also due to L. S. Summer for her well-crafted index.

For the image of the two-armed Avaloketeshvara, I am grateful to Lama Wangchen Phuntsog for his kindness in facilitating it so amazingly just in the nick of time, to Zashi Nima for beautifully painting it, and to Jim Rosen for refining the image.

Whatever benefit this book might bring is due to the blessings of the Buddha of Loving-Kindness and the kindness of friends. All the mistakes that have crept in are the reflections of my own ignorant shadow, for which I beg for forgiveness from the Buddha of Loving-Kindness and the forbearing readers.

The Heart of Unconditional Love

INTRODUCTION

When you remember the Lord Buddha of Loving-Kindness,
Your mind instantly becomes the mind of loving-kindness.
—SHAKYAMUNI BUDDHA

LOVING-KINDNESS IS THE ENTRYWAY to the unconditional love that we all long for—in our own hearts, in our relationships, and in the world around us. We define loving-kindness as the heartfelt wish for all beings to have happiness and the causes of happiness, and to put that wish into practice by serving all without self-interest. Loving-kindness enables us to serve others with dedication and authenticity. It is also one of the most effective ways to make ourselves truly happy now and in our future lives.

As it is commonly understood, loving-kindness does not necessarily include the wish that all beings attain enlightenment. However, in this book, I use *loving-kindness* to mean the wish that all beings have not only happiness, but also full enlightenment—Buddhahood. When used in this way, loving-kindness becomes what is called *bodhichitta* in Sanskrit. Developing this kind of loving-kindness, or bodhichitta, is the heart core of the Mahayana Buddhist trainings that lead us to enlightenment, and is central to the subject of this book.

A New Approach to Loving-Kindness Meditation

This book introduces a new way to meditate on loving-kindness, based on a four-stage structure. The approach is different from the usual practice in which the meditator begins by thinking lovingly about one single being and then expands that thought to include all beings. Although we will do that in this book as well, the key difference is that we begin by focusing on the unconditional love of the Buddha of Loving-Kindness. This Buddha, known as Avalokiteshvara in Sanskrit and as Chenrezi in Tibetan, embodies the qualities of all Enlightened Ones in one. Enlightened Ones are all the same in essence, even though they have different names and forms owing to followers' different needs and cultures.

With devotion and trust, we will bring the Buddha's love into our hearts, and from there we expand it gradually until it embraces infinite beings. The idea is similar to sunbathing. As our body absorbs the sun's heat, it becomes warm and gradually emanates that warmth into our surroundings. In the same way, through devotion and trust in the Buddha, we immerse our mind in his unconditional love, which we then radiate to those around us.

I have been fortunate to enjoy the unimaginable opportunities of growing up in Eastern Tibet at the feet of many true Masters of loving-kindness, who were amazing scholars and adepts of both exoteric (Sutra) and esoteric (Tantra) Buddhist teachings. Now I am engaging in the privilege of sharing a few drops of that wisdom that I was able to pick up with my own eyes, ears, and heart. Even today the memories of those fortunate times always fill my heart with never-ending wonder.

For decades I have been studying Buddhist teachings in general and especially meditations on devotion to the Buddhas and loving-kindness toward all beings. Gradually, over the years, I found that if I could understand the right methods of meditation on devotion and loving-kindness, and if I could earnestly put them into practice, the qualities and habits of my mind and life would slowly become more loving and joyful.

Then in recent years, it began to dawn on me that most Buddhist practices, such as those on devotion and loving-kindness, lead meditators through four distinct stages. The first stage, which I call the Outer Buddha, is to see the Buddha before oneself with devotion. The second stage, which I call the Inner Buddha, is to find the Buddha's unconditional love within oneself. The third stage, the Universal Buddha, is to awaken to the Buddha everywhere: the whole universe arises as his love. The fourth stage, the Ultimate Buddha, is to be in oneness with the Buddha's love. I talk about love because that's my subject here. But any enlightened quality could be substituted for it in this four-stage model. Although the Four Stages are conceptually distinct, each leads infallibly to the next. We can flow from one stage to another without needing to stop and shift gears.

I noticed that when I would regard a person (or any mental object) as embodying loving-kindness and appreciate them that way, then the thoughts and feelings of my own mind became thoughts and feelings of loving-kindness. As long as my mind was steeped in loving-kindness, whatever I saw, heard, or felt turned into phenomena of loving-kindness. The more I remained with thoughts of loving-kindness—as if I had become one with those feelings—the more perfect my experience of pure loving-kindness became. On the other hand, if I couldn't see or appreciate any qualities of loving-kindness in someone or something, but only related to them through negative feelings like hatred, greed, or jealousy, I never had a chance to manifest any loving-kindness in myself—not even for a moment.

I realized that, although Buddhism had been teaching these four stages throughout the ages, I was starting to understand them for the first time. I felt tremendous joy. The teachings do not make the stages explicit—but they are inherent. I believed that, if I could make the four stages explicit, meditators could focus on mastering each one at a time, making their progress effective and profound. So I came up with a new phrase—"the Four Buddha Stages"—in the hope that I might reach some other beginner Buddhist students like myself.

A number of friends in Tibet kept asking me for years to write something in Tibetan, as they knew that I had published many Dharma books in English over the past decades. They were aware that these books had been translated into quite a few languages, but not into Tibetan. So I finally wrote a short book in Tibetan, drawing on the Four Stages, on how to meditate on loving-kindness. The Tibetan title translates as "The Ornament of Motherly Love." In English the word *loving-kindness* is customarily used to translate the Sanskrit *maitri*, which means benevolent love, like the love of a mother who adores her child unconditionally. It is rare to find a person who has as much love as a mother does. The mother is renowned as the highest example of a person of loving-kindness. However, for the English version I changed the title to *The Heart of Unconditional Love* to hone in on the essence of loving-kindness.

My wife, Lydia Segal, and some Western friends urged me to translate the Tibetan book into English. However, I decided to write a new book directly in English. My purpose in writing this book is not to offer an intellectual text, show off my writing skills, or float any interesting new ideas. My goal is simply to present practices on loving-kindness in the format of a guided meditation to enable readers to directly experience the intrinsic essence of their own inherent loving-kindness. I am thrilled to offer this four-stage meditation formula to Western readers. It is profound in meaning, accessible to all, easy to understand, and effective in getting quick results. It distills the essential meditations and attainments of the whole of Mahayana Buddhism.

Summary of the Four Buddha Stages

1. In the Outer Buddha Stage, we open our hearts with devotion in prayer to the Buddha of Loving-Kindness. We see him as an external enlightened presence and feel his boundless power, omniscient wisdom, and especially his unconditional love, and then receive his blessings. This opens our mind to embodying his blessings and qualities in ourselves so that we can relate to the world with respect, appreciation, peace, joy, and especially loving-kindness.

The effectiveness of the Outer Buddha meditations is due both to the power of the Buddha of Loving-Kindness's blessings and to our own mind. Opening our heart to him with devotion unleashes enormous peace and joy in us. Of course, having devotion toward even an ordinary object or person will bring us peace and joy because it results from our own mind's positive perception. How much more so when the object of our devotion is a Buddha!

Although the Outer Buddha Stage is preliminary to the subsequent stages, that does not mean it is less important. In fact, it is extraordinary in itself. And without mastering it, we cannot reach the later stages effectively.

2. In the Inner Buddha Stage, we find the Buddha's love in our heart. Because we become what we see, think, and feel, our previous experience of the Outer Buddha's loving-kindness now awakens loving-kindness within ourselves. We then gradually expand our own loving-kindness, starting with one loved one until we reach infinite beings.

3. In the Universal Buddha Stage, we experience the whole universe as love. We develop the pure perception of perceiving everything as the images, sounds, and feelings of loving-kindness—the reflections of our own mind.

4. The Ultimate Buddha Stage is the realization of the ultimate state of "loving-kindness free from concepts." All dualistic concepts, afflicting emotions, and sensory thirsts gradually dissolve through the power of loving-kindness. We remain in the awareness of boundless loving-kindness free from concepts. This final stage is the result of all. If we realize the innate nature of loving-kindness, we realize the absolute nature of all.

A Few Questions

Throughout this book, I have tried my best to offer answers to some frequently asked questions: Why do we meditate on loving-kindness with devotion? Why do we say prayers? Why do we practice visualizations? How do we do them? Once we understand the reasons, benefits, and the formulas for doing these practices, we will naturally feel inspired to do them. Then we will surely be able to gain true meditation experiences and the various stages of beneficial results.

Here I will answer a few questions that may arise at the outset.

Why did you focus your book on loving-kindness instead of on compassion—given that so many Buddhist traditions focus on compassion?

In compassion meditations, people deeply feel the suffering of others and develop a strong wish to free them of it. When done with total openness, this meditation is a powerful way to awaken true inner strength, love, and peace. And if we have true compassion, we will automatically have loving-kindness as well.

However, I thought that, for some beginning meditators, meditating on others' suffering might be too painful and depressing. I personally know some Westerners who turned away from Buddhism because their initial introduction to it was through compassion meditations. They could not bear to dwell on the pain of their loved ones or the world.

Loving-kindness meditations, on the other hand, can only inspire. Also, once we progress in loving-kindness, we will inherently have compassion, too.

Why do you call Avalokiteshvara "the Buddha of Loving-Kindness" instead of "the Buddha of Compassion"?

The rough translation of the name Avalokiteshvara is "the Lord who watches over." He watches over all, all the time, with all-knowing wisdom, loving-kindness, and compassion. Many simply translate the name as "the Buddha of Compassion." But we can also call him, as I do in this book, "the Buddha of Loving-Kindness."

Why do we use dualistic meditations? Isn't the goal the non-dual state?

Yes, that is the goal; but we need to start our journey from where we are. Because we are conceptual, emotional beings, meditations that are conceptual and emotional are familiar to us. So it is relatively easy for us to use the power of positive concepts and feelings to transform our negative thoughts and feelings into positive ones. From there we can gradually reach perfection, or the nondual state. It is hard to leap from negative to perfection. It is much easier to go from positive to perfection. So, as we think about, feel, and enjoy the Buddha's loving-kindness, loving-kindness spontaneously awakens in our mindstream. Eventually, we discover that loving-kindness is, in fact, the ever-present nondual true nature of our mind.

What is the difference between loving-kindness and unconditional love?

Loving-kindness, as I use the phrase, is the wish for all to be happy and enlightened. Unconditional love is selfless love, the highest level of loving-kindness. When we first start meditating, we use concepts and emotions to make our loving-kindness less and less conditioned and more and more limitless. Eventually, we experience loving-kindness free from concepts. That is the perfection of unconditional love. It arises as the "wisdom of equality" of Buddhahood.

Opening Verse

O Buddha of Unconditional Love,
Your all-knowing wisdom eyes see all;
Your boundless power protects every being
As a mother protects her only child with
    unconditional love.

For he who sees the compassionate eyes of the
    Buddha of Loving-Kindness,
His own heart wakes up with the force of boundless
    devotion in the Buddha;
His own face blossoms with unconditional love for
    every mother-being.
I, a mere distant spectator, am imbued with awe-
    inspiring wonder.

Devotion to the Outer Buddha opens our heart as the
    heart of loving-kindness,
Transforming it into unconditional love for all, the
    Inner Buddha,
Awakening every image, sound, and feeling as the
    Universal Buddha, and

Uniting all as loving-kindness free from concepts, the
    Ultimate Buddha.

Sage of Great Accomplishments[1]—true image of
    loving-kindness—
Knowledge-holders,[2] Seekers of Enlightenment,[3] and
    Angels of Wisdom[4]—
I beseech you all from my heart-core with undying trust.
Please grant us your blessings to unite us indivisibly
    with you.

Infinite beings are caught in the wheel of endless
    cyclic existence,
Trapped in the eye of conceptual and emotional
    hurricanes,
Plunged in the midst of the turbulent waves of
    conflicting sensations,
Whirring around the world like bees—with no end to
    this nightmare in sight.

I have been wandering in many unknown lands for
    nearly sixty years.
But by the ever-present kindness of the Sage of Great
    Accomplishments,
And by the reminiscences of the Blazing Glorious
    Seat of Accomplishments,[5]
I haven't drifted too far from the light of the Dharma.

However great the sweetness of samsara is,
It cannot be compared with the joy of Dharma, by
    even a sixteenth.

However vehement the flame of evil deeds and the
   pain of samsara are,
There is none that the rain of Dharma cannot quench!

The brilliance of the sun-like Buddha's love
   illuminates the sky.
The radiance of our mighty ocean-like devotion
   embraces it.
The glow of earth and sky unite into a single world of
   boundless joy.
This is the true meditation on devotion to the Buddha
   of Loving-Kindness.

Avalokiteshvara, noble lord of omniscient wisdom,
Is always looking at us with eyes of loving-kindness.
Whenever we see him with devotion, the
   unconditional love of his heart
Awakens in us, miraculously. This is what I adore to
   articulate in this book.

Exceedingly destitute in both learning and
   realization, I fear that
My attempt to write about loving-kindness will be a
   cause of laughter—even to my own tongue.
Nevertheless, to not let some drops trickle forth from
   the miraculous ocean of loving-kindness is harder
   for me to bear.
O learned readers, please forgive me for my pitiable
   flops.

PART ONE

VIEW

*What Is Loving-Kindness
and How to Develop It*

1

THE IMPORTANCE OF
TRAINING OUR MIND

THE WORLD WITH EVERYTHING in it that appears to us is created and perceived as such by our own conceptual mind, and shared by all beings with whom we have mental habits in common. That is why, in this book, we are going to be training our mind to develop loving-kindness. If we can improve our mental qualities by developing loving-kindness, then the world will reflect back to us as a world of love and peace.

The True Nature of Mind

To understand how the world can be a creation of the mind, it is useful to recognize that our mind has two aspects: ordinary mind and enlightened mind. Ordinary mind, also known in Mahayana teachings as deluded mind, is conceptual, dualistic, and emotional. Enlightened mind—also known as the awakened state or Buddha-nature—is the true and pure nature of the mind. For most of us, the dualistic concepts, unhealthy emotions, and obsessive sensations (particularly strong clinging and craving) of our ordinary mind cover the enlightened aspect of our mind. These thoughts are like coverings that obstruct us from realizing and manifesting our true nature—like clouds covering the sun.

Consider the difference between how an awakened person and an ordinary person view a flower. When an awakened person sees a flower, they see it through their enlightened wisdom-eyes that are free from the shrouds of duality, emotions and sensations, and that dwell instead in the nature of boundless openness, also known as "emptiness" nature. By contrast, when an ordinary person sees a flower, they see it through the eyes of their deluded mind, which is characterized by duality. Duality leads to attachment and aversion, which, as they become increasingly tight and obsessive, result in the familiar cycle of fireworks and misery.

With realized persons, the subject, the object, and experience arise fully as the awareness wisdom of ultimate peace and openness. That is the view of "absolute truth," the true nature.

With ordinary persons, the person (subject), the flower (object), and the experience of seeing (action) all remain separate, conceptual, and dualistic. That is the perspective of "relative truth." Thus, to the ordinary person, everything that exists, everything that happens, is seen through conceptual lenses. The person's perception is false because it is merely a projection, a reflection, an illusion, and a fabrication of their conceptual mind. That is why the Buddha said:

> Due to the waves of conceptual habits,
> Mind arises in various forms and
> Mental objects appear as external phenomena.

The whole of samsara is just mind.
External appearances do not exist.
They are the mind appearing in various forms.
So I tell you, everything is just mind![6]

We can get an inkling of how our mind affects our perception even in our everyday lives. For instance, when we struggle with difficulties, if our attitude is positive, we find that our pain is less and we are more at ease. And we can see that happy people are happy not because of material or external circumstances, but because of the peace and strength of their own mind. The Third Dodrupchen[7] writes:

Wise people realize that all happiness and suffering depend upon the mind, and [so they] seek happiness from the mind itself. They do not rely on external sources, as they understand that the causes of happiness are complete within themselves. If we realize this, then whether we face problems caused by other beings or material things, they won't be able to hurt us much at all.[8]

In fact, our mind can radically improve our world because the enlightened nature is inherent in our mind at this very moment, even if we can't see it because it is covered by the deluded aspect of our mind. Every being has this potential, regardless of whether we are a human being or an animal, let alone whether we are a Buddhist. Maitreya-natha[9] writes:

The [ultimate] body of the Buddha pervades [all].
The ultimate nature is [in all] without distinction.
All beings have the lineage [of becoming Buddha].
Beings always possess Buddha-nature.[10]

However, we need to train our ordinary mind to dispel its illusory concepts and unveil our enlightened mind. In this effort, our mind is our principal tool, the main player, both the aspirant and beneficiary. After all, what covers our enlightened nature? Who attains enlightenment? Our mind. The Buddha became enlightened through his own meditation, for meditation directly, instantly, and fully affects the mind—since the mind is the one meditating. So the mind is what we use to follow the path out of delusion and attain the goal, Buddhahood. At the same time, the path and goal lie in the mind itself.

Although with the right meditation we can transform our mind into infinite virtues, our body, in contrast, no matter how much we train it, will always be bounded by more rigidly set physical parameters—unless we transform it into a "wisdom-light body" through unique esoteric mind training. However, such training is not my subject here, and not my cup of tea anyway.

When Our Mind Becomes Loving, Everything Else Does Too

If we train our mind to become peaceful and loving, then whatever we say and do will be peaceful and loving, and will inspire peace and joy in those around us. For example, if we see or think about a positive image, sound, or feeling and perceive it as beneficial, the effects of that perception will be a helpful influence for our mind, as it is being transformed into a mind of positive thoughts and feelings with the support of that beneficial object. Say we are in a garden, appreciating its peace and beauty; our mind will naturally become relaxed and joyful. The more peaceful our mind becomes, the more it will be filled with joy. Then our vocal and physical expressions will also spontaneously become caring and soothing for others. All our actions will become sources of true service for everyone we engage with.

How true this is, especially when what we are seeing and appreciating is the amazing presence of the Buddha of Loving-Kindness with his extraordinary qualities! Then, by his blessing power, by the positive power of our mind with its positive perception, and by the power of our meditation and prayer, our mind will become peaceful, joyful, and healthy. All our mental, vocal, and physical acts will turn into sources of truly helpful blessings for ourselves and others. Buddha Shakyamuni said:

Mind leads phenomena.
Mind is the main factor and forerunner of all.
If one speaks or acts with a pure mind,
One enjoys happiness, just as a shadow follows its
    object. . . .
By preserving mindfulness,
If you tame and discipline your mind, you
    experience joy.
People who safeguard their minds
Will certainly attain cessation of suffering.[11]

We don't need laboratory experiments, fancy machines, or scholarly investigations to verify this. It is plain, understandable, and natural. However, scientific studies of the benefits of compassion and loving-kindness meditation have been conducted. (See, for example, the research reported by Daniel Goleman in the book *Destructive Emotions.*)

So let us train our minds in meditation to free ourselves from the struggles of relative truth and attain absolute truth. If we do so, then our deeds, behaviors, and their consequences will follow our mind's lead. As the Buddha said:

> All deeds depend on the mind.
> Their effects depend on the mind.
> Similarly, the mind appears in various
>   characteristics,
> As do its effects.
> The three existents [three worlds] follow the mind.
> All are drawings of the mind.
> There is nothing that is not controlled by the mind.
> Mind is the basis and cause of
> Both bondage and liberation.
> Virtuous deeds liberate beings.
> Unvirtuous deeds bind them.
> Thus beings wander in the three existents,
> Driven by the force of their minds.[12]

The Buddha's First Teachings: The Four Noble Truths

The Buddha set forth the importance of training the mind more than twenty-five centuries ago, when he gave his first teaching to his first five disciples at Deer Park, now known as Sarnath, about eight miles from the ancient city of Varanasi in North India. The teaching was on the Four Noble Truths, which became the foundation and essence of Buddhism. The Buddha taught that if we train our minds in the right way, our confusion and suffering will cease, and happiness and eventually full enlightenment, freedom from suffering, will result. The Buddha said:

> O Monks, there are Four Noble Truths. They are the Noble Truths of Suffering, the Cause of Suffering, the Freedom from Suffering, and the Path to the Freedom from Suffering.[13]

The Buddha taught that there is nothing in this mundane world but suffering. Life is full of pain. Nothing can be relied upon, because everything is temporary. That is the First Noble Truth of Suffering. We must recognize this as it is, and determine to be liberated from this ocean of misery.

The cause of our suffering, the Buddha explained, is our negative deeds, whether physical, vocal, or mental. These deeds leave habitual traces in our mind. These traces, in turn, produce commensurate experiences for us in the future. This chain of cause and effect is called karma. At the root of karma is the duality of deluded mind. As long as we remain in the never-ending cycle of lives created by negative causes and effects, and as long as our minds are ignorant of the truth, we keep wandering endlessly and aimlessly around samsara—cyclic existence. This is the Second Noble Truth. We must recognize it and stop engaging in deeds that will cause us future pain.

The Buddha then taught that there is a state where all suffering ends. That state is enlightenment or Buddhahood. This is the state where we realize the true nature of our mind and the universe, as it is—nondual and free from all trace of concepts or emotions. This is the Third Noble Truth. We must attain it.

Then the Buddha taught something radical: there is a path that leads to enlightenment. Buddhists call it the Eightfold Noble Path. It gives us the tools—right view, right thought, right speech, right action, right livelihood, right effort, right mindfulness, and right concentration— to purify our heart and attain Buddhahood. If we pursue the path of positive thoughts and deeds, we will improve the quality of our existence. And if we realize perfect wisdom, we will attain freedom from suffering and Buddhahood, the cessation of cyclic existence. This is the Fourth Noble Truth. We must apply it to our hearts.

Uprooting Ignorance and Awakening Wisdom

Shakyamuni Buddha said that he attained enlightenment by, among other things, meditating on how we enter cyclic existence and on reversing that process. He said that we enter cyclic existence through the "twelve links of interdependent arising." This cycle is rooted in ignorance. It matures into an endless chain of turbulent life cycles immersed in suffering and fed by grasping, craving, and clinging. The Buddha said:

What are the twelve links of interdependent arising? Because of ignorance, formation [karma] arises.

Because of formation, consciousness arises.

Because of consciousness, the mental components and body arise.

Because of the mental components and body, the six sense bases arise.

Because of the six sense-bases, contact [between them] arises.

Because of contact, feeling arises.

Because of feeling, craving arises.

Because of craving, clinging arises.

Because of clinging, becoming arises.

Because of becoming, birth takes place.

Because of birth, old age, death, sorrow, lamentations, suffering, sadness, and conflicts take place.[14]

The Buddha meditated on the reversal that brings the chain of these twelve links to an end. He said:

The cessation of ignorance causes the cessation of formation. . . . The cessation of birth causes the cessation of old age, death, sorrow . . . and the whole great heap of suffering.[15]

Through this meditation, the Buddha realized that there is no "self" as a truly existing reality, but just the emptiness or openness nature, where all arises and ceases through mere dependence on causes and conditions—like a mirage. The Buddha said:

Those bodhisattvas who have attained the wisdom of realizing

The [union of] interdependent arising and the unborn
    and unceasing [nature of emptiness],
Like rays of the unclouded sun dispelling darkness,
Destroy ignorance and attain naturally present
    [Buddhahood].[16]

Having attained enlightenment, the Buddha pro-
claimed:

Profound and peaceful luminosity that is
    uncompounded and free from concepts,
A nectar-like attainment—I have realized![17]

*Loving-Kindness Meditations Accomplish the Path That the
Buddha Set Forth*

If we meditate on loving-kindness toward all beings from
the bottom of our heart with devotion toward the Buddha,
we will spontaneously be training in and perfecting the
Eightfold Noble Path and the reversal of the twelve links of
interdependent arising.

By training in the first three Buddha Stages of loving-kindness meditations in this book, we generate positive causation through positive thoughts and deeds, and
bring true peace and love into our mindstream. By training in the meditations in the Fourth Buddha Stage, we can
eventually awaken the nature of our mind, loving-kindness
free from concepts. Then, by realizing the union of wisdom
and loving-kindness, we can attain liberation from ignorance. The cycle of the twelve links of interdependent arising, with all its sensory thirst, attachment, and suffering,

will end for us. We will attain the fully enlightened state, Buddhahood, with its three bodies and five wisdoms.

So let us exert ourselves to awaken our heart of loving-kindness and turn all thoughts, senses, feelings, and deeds into the boundless energies of loving-kindness, joy, devotion, trust, and service for all. Then every step of our life will be a source of openness, peace, and joy for ourselves and others and will lead toward the realization of enlightenment. As Konchog Dronme[18] advises:

> You must develop great compassion by thinking of all the beings who are suffering in the chain of the twelve links of interdependent arising from beginningless time.[19]

2

ESSENTIAL TOOLS
FOR MEDITATION

JUST AS WE NEED TOOLS to build a house, so, too, do we need tools to meditate on loving-kindness. The four essential tools for meditation are positive images, positive words or thoughts, positive feelings and experiences, and trust. All meditations use these four tools (with the exception of contemplative meditations free from concepts).

Four Essential Tools

1. *Positive images.* If we keep gazing at a positive image, such as a flower or a picture of a good friend, and if we recognize its positive qualities and stay with that positive view, that will start to turn the chain of our thoughts, and eventually our whole life, into a cycle of peace and joy. Getting into the habit of visualizing or imagining positive objects and recognizing and enjoying their positive qualities will be enormously helpful to us, because it works directly on the mind, which generates, maintains, and enjoys the training. Once our mind is trained in imagining (or visualizing) positive sources of blessing, we can conjure them up any time, any place. We could turn all our free time into the cycle of this training, wherever we may be. And once we

taste the benefits of this practice, we will want very much to spend our free time in this way.

The most powerful positive images are ones with spiritual meaning and power, such as images of the Buddha of Loving-Kindness and his Pure Land—the paradise of peace and joy that he created to liberate beings. Seeing them as a source of loving-kindness and an object of devotion will become highly meaningful and effective.

One thing we should watch out for is grasping, getting attached to or becoming aggressive about a positive object. Instead, we should approach these objects with a sense of openness, appreciation, peace, joy, confidence, and love.

2. *Positive words or thoughts.* Positive words or thoughts that describe or convey the positive images that we are seeing help us to define, generate, focus, illuminate, and amplify their positive qualities and effects. If we could turn all words and labels into positive ones, we could turn our whole life into a cycle of positive energy and waves: expressions of the qualities of positive phenomena, from our heart and from the core of the cells of our body. Prayers to the Buddha of Loving-Kindness, which have spiritual significance, are the most profound positive words and sounds.

3. *Positive feelings and experiences.* Feeling respect and appreciation for the positive qualities of the images, thoughts, and words that we enjoy makes an especially deep impact on our life, turning it into a wheel of the energy of joy and peace, and maximizing their beneficial effects. When we use feelings, we don't just see a positive image externally or think about it with our intellect: we actually experience, enjoy, and unite with its healthy qualities, such as peace and joy. Feeling loving-kindness (that is, wishing

joy for all beings) and feeling devotion (that is, opening our heart with joyful energy and trust in the wisdom, love, and power of the Buddha) are the most powerful and effective trainings to realize and perfect high spiritual attainments.

4. *Trusting in positive objects and qualities.* Trusting here means having confidence in the presence and power of positive images, thoughts, and feelings. Trust accomplishes and seals their positive power firmly and perfects their positive results fully. If we want to transform our ordinary intellectual and emotional life into a life of spiritual attainment and Buddha qualities, it is important that we trust in the sources of blessings: the Buddha of Loving-Kindness and his qualities; the meditation of loving-kindness; the power of Buddha's blessings; the effects of meritorious deeds; and the power of one's own mind of loving-kindness. Guru Rinpoche (Padmasambhava)[20] explained the importance of trust:

> O my followers who are wishing to leave samsara
>   behind:
> Continuously pray to me with trust and devotion.
> One-pointedly pray with the melody of
> Moving waves, poignantly like an infant calling its
>   parents
> In a voice as sweet as if it were the sound of a flute.
> Pray six times—every day and night. . . .
> Trust will develop when you see the benefits.
> You will receive the blessings if you have the "thou
>   knowest" trust.
> Your wishes will be accomplished if you have no
>   doubts.[21]

Once we enjoy spiritual attainments, such as unconditional love, with confidence and trust, our mind will have secured and perfected the four positive tools.

We will use all these tools in the meditations on loving-kindness. In the Outer Buddha Stage, for instance, we see, think about, and feel the Buddha's enlightened qualities from the heart. We hear and sing his Six-Syllable Prayer (see below). We develop trust in him from the depth of our heart, believing that he is not just an image we conjured up, but the true living presence of the Buddha of Loving-Kindness before us. We also trust in the spiritual capacity of our mind as well.

Three Key Qualities: Wisdom, Love, and Power

A Tibetan proverb says, "All activity is imitation. Whoever best imitates an activity will be the best at that activity." So whatever qualities of the Buddha we choose to focus on, we will inherit.

The Buddha has countless qualities. For the purposes of our meditations, however, we will be concerned with three key qualities declared in these words of the *Uttara Tantra:* "Buddha embodies wisdom, love, and power."[22] In our meditations we will be seeing, thinking about, feeling, and trusting the Buddha's omniscient wisdom, unconditional love, and boundless power.

In so doing, we will be receiving the Buddha's blessings *through* and *as* these three qualities. The more alive and vivid we can make them, the more our mind will awaken. Shakyamuni Buddha said that if we keep thinking about the Buddha's qualities, we will attain them. A sutra says:

> As long as you remain in this world, you must hear the names, prayers, and virtues of the Buddhas, such as the Buddha of Infinite Life. And you must recall them in your mind, again and again. As the result, you will be able to see the Buddhas, such as the Buddha of Infinite Life, and be able to make your entreaties. By the power of thinking of the Buddha, you generate the forces of virtuous deeds, develop meditative absorptions, and gain the opportunity to see him.[23]

When we see the loving presence of the Buddha and enjoy his loving-kindness, an uncontrived and unconditional thought of loving-kindness—a strong wish for all beings to have peace, joy, and full enlightenment—will clearly take birth in our mind. The Third Dodrupchen writes:

> By just seeing the face of [the Buddha],
> Beings develop virtuous deeds.
> By just seeing the sun[-like Buddha],
> Beings' lotus-like eyes of joy blossom.[24]

When we contemplate the Buddha's qualities of body, speech, and mind, we should not perceive them as objects to grasp at, ideas to conceptualize, or sensory experiences to get attached to. Instead, we should see and appreciate them with fully open senses and our mind's boundlessly blossoming energies of devotion. This way of perceiving and enjoying awakens and imprints these enlightened qualities in us. Every physical, vocal, and wisdom quality of the Buddha that we enjoy reflects our own true physical, vocal, and wisdom qualities.

Blessed Words, Sacred Sounds: The Six-Syllable Prayer

We will also use blessed words and sacred sounds in the meditations. Although it is perfectly fine to use our own words to give expression to the earnest feelings of our devotional hearts, we will be saying a traditional mantra, the Six-Syllable Prayer, to the Buddha of Loving-Kindness: OM MA-NI PAD-ME HUNG.[25] With devotional energy, we will repeatedly chant or sing it in the sweetest voice and melody from the depth of our fully blossoming mind, heart, and body. We pray with the waves of our voice unlocked by the flood of our devotional energy, without any hesitation or cessation, like the never-ceasing flow of a calm river.

We can also simply pray by saying the Buddha's name: "O Avalokiteshvara."[26] His name has great significance and blessing power to ease suffering. Shantideva[27] writes:

> The Lord Avalokiteshvara
> With great loving-kindness
> Has blessed even his name
> To dispel the fears of samsara.[28]

Avalokiteshvara's name in Tibetan is Chenrezi. Explaining the meaning of his name, the Third Dodrupchen writes:

> There are two ways to interpret it: [He] who always sees [the whole universe as] naturally pure with his all-knowing wisdom eyes. Or [he] who spontaneously sees the whole universe with the eyes of great loving-kindness.[29]

Patrul Rinpoche[30] teaches how to say the mantra of the Six-Syllable Prayer:

> The root of the Mahayana path is bodhichitta.
> This sublime thought is the sole path taken by the Buddhas.
> Never departing from the excellent path of bodhichitta
> And compassion to all beings—recite the Six Syllables. . . .
> The one deity in which all the Buddhas are embodied is Avalokiteshvara.
> The one mantra in which the essences of all esoteric practices are condensed is the Six Syllables.
> The one meditation in which both the development and perfection stages are condensed is bodhichitta.
> Through the state of knowing the One that liberates all—recite the Six Syllables. . . .
> The true state of all phenomenal existents is Dharmakaya, pure from the beginning.
> If you see the true face of Dharmakaya, that is Avalokiteshvara.

Avalokiteshvara is not somewhere else.
Through the state of realizing all as pure, recite the
　　Six Syllables. . . .
When concepts of dual obscurations are pacified,
　　then the experiences and realizations will be
　　developed.
When you gain control over your mind, then all foes
　　and forces will be tamed.
Avalokiteshvara is the one who grants these common
　　and uncommon attainments in this very lifetime.
In the state of spontaneous accomplishment of the
　　four actions[31]—recite the Six Syllables. . . .
Mind is the gathering of the eight consciousnesses.
If you realize the nature of the mind as the
　　Dharmakaya, that is Avalokiteshvara.
The ocean of the noble Buddhas is not somewhere
　　else.
In the state of realizing your mind as the Buddha—
　　recite the Six Syllables.[32]

So sing the Six-Syllable Prayer as a way of calling the
Buddha for his kind attention, care, protection, and blessings.

Sing the prayer to celebrate the dawn of loving-kindness of the Buddha in your heart and in all.

Sing the prayer to unite with and remain inseparable
from the ultimate nature of the loving-kindness of the
Buddha.

Receiving Blessing Lights

We will be receiving and experiencing the Buddha's wisdom and love in the form of "blessing lights" to purify and transform ourselves mentally and physically. The blessings can be seen as light or nectar of light. (See chapter 14 for a visualization of nectar of light.) As the Third Dodrupchen writes:

> While [one is] receiving empowerments, the rays of light in white, red, blue, and so on, should be seen as the appearances of blissful nectar in the form of light.[33]

These lights emanate from the Buddha's body and from the syllables of the mantra. Likening the syllables of the mantra to the beads of the rosary, or *mala,* Patrul Rinpoche writes:

> From the *mala* of syllables, a nectar of wisdom and love cascades.[34]

The lights also emanate from the Buddha's Pure Land, which is inseparable from his wisdom. Chechog Dondrub Tsal[35] explains about the Pure Land:

> It is the wisdom-mind of the Buddha
> Appearing as the mandala.[36]

Wisdom-Light

The Pure Land is made of wisdom-light. As Karma Lingpa[37] describes: "The palace [of the Buddha Pure Land] is made of five wisdom-lights."[38]

In common Buddhist teachings (the Sutra tradition), the Buddha's blessing lights are like external agents that purify and elevate us, eventually leading us to Buddhahood. In esoteric Buddhist teachings (Tantra), the lights don't operate as external agents. Rather, by receiving blessing lights, we unite with them, perfecting ourselves as the very body of the Buddha's wisdom, love, and power. We should choose whichever practice best suits our abilities and training. The Buddha said:

> The Buddha fills as many worlds as the number of
>   grains of sand of the Ganges River with lights that
>   come from his body.
> Whoever is touched by these lights is assured to
>   attain Full Enlightenment.[39]

Shantarakshita[40] says that the Buddha's lights heal us and lead us to liberation:

> The Supreme Physician [Buddha] heals the sickness
>   of beings.
> His complexion is as bright as lapis.
> The lights of his body liberate beings.
> O King of Healers—to you I pay homage.[41]

Conveying the tantric understanding of how the blessing lights operate, Pema Ledreltsal writes:

> The pure perception of wisdom is seeing things as
>   they dwell in their true nature—suchness.
> They are the objects of wisdom.
> [All] existents arise as the play of Buddha bodies and
>   wisdom.[42]

When we receive blessing lights, we experience that every particle of our body and every aspect of our mind is filled with joyful or blissful heat, which is the light of loving-kindness. If we enjoy and remain in that experience, all our unvirtuous thoughts and pain will gradually ease and completely dissolve. Before long, an experience of a new, uncommon blissful heat of loving-kindness will take birth in us and start to grow. "Wisdom-light" is also known as "the natural light of wisdom" and "the radiance of wisdom."[43] It has an absolute and a relative meaning:

Absolute meaning: In its true nature, our mind remains fully open as all-knowing wisdom. Objects remain as wisdom's radiance itself. In this unity—of our mind and the world (objects)—all remain as openness and ever-radiant. This unity is "wisdom-light." It is how Buddha and the Buddha Pure Land, Buddha and Buddha blessings, are present in absolute union. This unity transcends all dimension and color. The *Trashi Dzeden* tantra says:

> The awareness [wisdom] is present with great clarity
> like the five [colored] lights. However, [as it is empti-
> ness,] there are no colors to be distinguished.[44]

Relative meaning: For most of us, this absolute view is hard to realize. It is easier to approach it through meditations on relative meaning—pure perception. So we must see and feel the Buddha with all-knowing wisdom, the world as his Pure Land, and his blessings as the pure light and nectar emanating from his wisdom.

Ordinarily, our mind is the subject, the grasper; and the gross phenomena that we perceive are the objects. As our mind sees and feels mental objects, dualistic concepts arise, followed by craving and clinging, clashes and conflicts, actions and reactions, resulting in endless cycles of birth and rebirth in suffering.

If, instead, we meditate on pure perception—seeing the Buddha and his Pure Land of light and unconditional love—we will refine our rigid mental concepts into softer, brighter, and more loving and open qualities. One day, we will see and enjoy the world as a pure land of light and love. Eventually, these pure-perception meditations will lead us to perfect the absolute "wisdom-light."

3

DEVOTION AND TRUST
The Keys to Loving-Kindness

THE TWO KEYS TO DEVELOPING loving-kindness in this book are devotion toward and trust in the Buddha of Loving-Kindness. Devotion in general refers to liking, wanting, yearning, and being inspired by and dedicated to the object of our devotion. In fact, devotion lies at the root of many things we accomplish, because we need to be dedicated in order to succeed. That's why the root of all virtue is said to be devotion in virtue and the sources of virtue. Shantideva writes:

> The Buddha said:
> The root of all virtuous deeds
> Is devotion.[45]

In the context of our meditation, devotion is the energy of opening our heart with the joy of being in the Buddha's presence and wanting or yearning to be in his aura of loving-kindness.

Devotion generally embodies trust and, at the same time, is the means to generate and perfect trust.[46] To trust something is to fully know and believe it on the basis of our understanding and experience.

There are different degrees of trust: (1) clear, joyous, or inspirational trust; (2) yearning trust; (3) confident trust; and (4) irreversible trust.[47] Jigme Lingpa[48] describes these different levels of trust:

> If, as soon as you see a teacher or read the scriptures,
> The hairs of your body stand straight like trees.
> That is joyous clarity, the first trust.
> There are also yearning, confident, and irreversible
>   trusts.
> However, when you are going for refuge,
> You must have trust that is irreversible—that is, even
>   at the cost of your life.[49]

How to Develop Devotion and Trust

Like any other skill, devotion and trust require commitment and effort to develop. We should start by cultivating devotion. If we have strong devotion in the Buddha, that devotion will eventually turn into perfect trust.

How can we develop devotion? The usual way, according to tradition, is to contemplate the frightening miseries of mundane life versus the joy of liberation. Shantideva writes:

> Devotion develops by thinking about the fear of
>   suffering
> And the benefits of [liberation].[50]

However, in the meditations that we are learning here, devotion begins with inspiration. This is a more effortless way, because when we are inspired by something, we like it. Then we want it and yearn for it. And then we get excited by and committed to it.

We then use the four tools (described in chapter 2) to think about, see, and feel the Buddha's awe-inspiring qualities—his omniscient wisdom, his boundless power, and especially his unconditional love for us and for all beings. We need to feel his presence from the depth of our heart. We should communicate with him. We can pray to him like a thirsty child calling for her mother from the depth of her heart; and we can pray to him with the boundless joy of celebration for being in his loving presence—both of which we do in the Outer Buddha Stage. Then, after a while, whenever we remember him, we will feel his qualities more vividly and our heart will be filled with joy and longing for him and his qualities.

How can we develop trust? Trust grows as we experience the benefits of meditation and find the Buddha inside and outside of us. Guru Rinpoche said:

Trust will develop when you see the benefits.[51]

So we need to continue to spend "quality time" with the Buddha, dwelling in his extraordinary qualities and receiving and experiencing his blessings again and again. Je Tsongkhapa writes:

If, through various methods, you remember the merits of the Buddha, trust will be developed in many ways. If you remember his merits again and again, the energy of your trust will become stronger and more durable.[52]

Jigme Lingpa mentions remembering the Three Jewels—the Buddha, Dharma, and Sangha—as one of the four ways to develop trust:

> There are four causes of developing trust—
> Relying on a holy person(s),
> Associating with holy friends,
> Remembering the Three Jewels, and
> Contemplating the faults and meaninglessness of
> samsara.[53]

The well-known Buddhist scholar D. T. Suzuki explains the effects of saying prayers from the heart, in his discussion of the Pure Land tradition as it is practiced in East Asia. He writes that "love and compassion are experienced when NAMU-AMIDA-BUTSU is pronounced with singleness of heart."[54] (This is the prayer to the Buddha of Infinite Light in Japanese.)

Eventually, by the power of repeatedly praying to the Buddha with one-pointed devotion and trust, our mind will fill with total confidence and trust whenever we remember him and his loving-kindness. Our heart fills with limitless joy and bliss, and our body fills with the healing warmth of blissful heat. This experience opens our heart and karmic doors as wide as the limitless sky when the clouds disperse. The experience further strengthens and amplifies our trust and confidence in the Buddha and his unconditional love from the depth and wholeness of our mind. These experiences stimulate energy waves of ever-greater joy that infuse every aspect of our mind, and waves of blissfulness that infuse every corner of every particle of our body. The powerful energy of this kind of devotion causes every particle of our body and every thought to become boundlessly open and totally free, like the immensely open clear sky.

A classic example of great devotion is the encounter between Tagtu Ngu, the bodhisattva known as "Ever Weeping," and the great Master Chöphag, the Noble One. Shakyamuni Buddha retells what Tagtu Ngu said about Chöphag.[55]

> As soon as I saw the Noble One teaching Dharma,
> I felt that same intense bliss that a monk experiences when he enters into the first stage of meditative absorption.[56]

Devotion and trust are self-reinforcing. As they fill our minds, we become increasingly aware of the flood of Buddha blessings and loving-kindness permeating our mind and body, and transforming everything into a universe of devotion, wishing happiness and enlightenment for all. It is just as when we open the doors and windows to our room, and the sunlight floods in. This makes it easy for us to develop even stronger trust and many other virtues. Longchen Rabjam[57] writes:

> The nature of trust is like a fertile land.
> It is the ground of Dharma, the cause of virtues flourishing.[58]

How to Deal with Doubt and Uncertainty

Sometimes we may face doubt, or feel uncertain and hesitant. This confusion is rooted in our dualistic grasping at "self" and grasping at unwholesome things. The Buddha's real form cannot be perceived by dualistic eyes or touched by physical senses. We have to find a way to ease our doubts and hesitations and find reasons to trust, believe in, and appreciate the Buddha.

If we are not sure that the Buddha can really help us, we should remember that many followers have enjoyed his blessings and presence and had their needs fulfilled by his enlightened actions. We also need to contemplate his qualities. He has all the qualities that we can rely on, appreciate, love, and know will benefit us. So there is no reason to entertain doubts about his trustworthiness and power to help us.

If we have doubts about the Buddha's very existence, we should first remember that whatever our mind sees and thinks, that is our reality. If we see someone as a person of peace and joy, we will receive benefits accordingly. So even if there were no Buddha, we would still benefit from believing in him. And if there is a Buddha, we certainly benefit. So we should try to appreciate and contemplate him in order to benefit ourselves, as millions of other people do and have done.

Third, we must remember that the Buddha is equated with the "absolute truth"—the true nature and universal goodness. Even if we do not believe in the Buddha according to the way he is traditionally depicted, we can probably believe in universal goodness and unconditional love. If so, we should see, feel, and experience these qualities until we have a spiritual experience of becoming intimate with them. Then we should dwell in that experience. That's how to establish trust. We can understand the Buddha as *being* that universal pure nature and those pure qualities. So in the end, it is up to us to acquire trust and obtain benefits.

As our trust and devotion grow, they dissolve all the doubts and questions of our wavering, flickering, wary minds without a trace. It will feel like such a relief, such freedom.

While every being has Buddha mind, for beginners like me it is essential to have a blessed presence with enlightened qualities like the Buddha of Loving-Kindness as the object of devotion and trust, rather than an ordinary person with mundane qualities. Because our minds do not yet have the irreversible force of pure perception, we could easily become attracted to and grasp at the mundane qualities of ordinary people or objects. This would lead to a host of negative emotions such as attachment, hatred, disappointment, confusion, and hurt. We'd end up angry and sad, and would fail to fulfill our goals.

On the other hand, relying on a Buddha and his qualities will never be a cause for disappointment or sadness. The Buddha will never abandon us and will never change. All we need to do is turn our mind to him, and there he is. When our hearts open to the Buddha with trust and devotion, his presence and blessings will be in and with us wherever we are, whatever we are doing—like space, which never leaves us. He will always be there, returning our loving gaze with unconditional love, the ever-present source of peace and joy. Just knowing that we are in his presence will fill us with joy and loving-kindness.

The very instant our mind fills with the feeling of the Buddha's love, it transforms into a mind of love, peace, and joy. Then how could we possibly feel unhappy or doubtful?

All we need to do is remember to look at him and enjoy his qualities with an open mind, without grasping at him or being attached to him. Then his presence will lead us from happiness to happiness.

The Results of Devotion and Trust

Having devotion and trust produces enormous virtue, peace, and joy within us. It also sparks the wish to serve infinite beings with immense dynamism, to ease their suffering and help them attain enlightenment. Just as the warmth of the sunlight causes infinite flowers on the earth to blossom simultaneously, so does the heat of devotion to the Buddha of Loving-Kindness cause us to instantly and spontaneously generate a strong, heartfelt thought of wishing joy for all.

If we keep remembering the Buddha and his loving-kindness with devotion and trust, we will be guided by him all the time and will develop bodhichitta. The Buddha said:

> Whoever has trust in the Buddha and in the Buddha's
>   teachings
> Has trust in the deeds of the offspring of the Buddha
> And has trust in the supreme bodhichitta.
> They will develop the Mind of the Great Beings
>   [bodhichitta].[59]

Having devotion and trust in the Buddha and his loving-kindness results in attaining incomparable peace. The Buddha said:

Monks who maintain loving-kindness and
Have trust in the teachings of the Buddha
Will attain a state of peace
That is inconceivable.[60]

Devotion and trust in the Buddha will lead to liberation. The Buddha said:

While walking, sitting, standing, or sleeping,
Whoever remembers the moon-like Buddha,
The Buddha will be present in front of that person.
The Buddha will cause him or her to attain nirvana.[61]

The power of trust and devotion will ultimately awaken in us enlightened mind, unconditional love, and the realization of suchness, the absolute nature of our mind. The Buddha said:

Having fully developed everlasting trust, a clear
    mind, and devotion
In all the Buddhas, the Dharma, and the Noble Ones,
He who makes offerings to the teacher with respect
Will develop the enlightened mind.
Whoever has trust in the Buddha and the Buddha's
    teaching, and
Whoever has trust in the activities of the Buddha and
    the bodhisattvas,
Will enjoy confidence in unexcelled enlightenment.
The mind of great beings will take birth in them. . . .
Trust causes your mind to be fully inspired by the
    Dharma.

Trust elevates your wisdom and qualities.
Trust shows you Buddhahood and facilitates your
    attaining it. . . .
Those who have vast trust
Will always be blessed by the Buddha.
In those who are blessed by the Buddha,
Bodhichitta will take birth. . . .
Whoever enjoys unshakable remembrance of the
    Buddha
Will always see inconceivable numbers of Buddhas.[62]

Maitreya-natha also says:

The spontaneously present ultimate truth
Can be realized through trust alone.
If you don't have the eyes [of trust],
You won't even see the body of the sun, radiant with
    light.[63]

Again, Maitreya-natha says:

If you meditate on virtuous qualities such as trust,
The Fully Enlightened One will appear in your mind
With noble signs and excellent marks. . . .
Beings will witness
The display of various miracles—
The great deeds and splendors [of the Buddha].
Having seen such display, enthusiasts
Will designate him as the very Buddha.[64]

John Blofeld, a British writer on Asian religion, gives
a modern account of the power of such trust.[65] A Taiwan-

ese official confessed to Blofeld that he was once driven to act on an impulse to kill his abusive stepmother. But when she saw him approach, she prayed aloud to Kuan Yin, the Buddha of Loving Kindness in female form. The man, his hands raised to attack, found himself suddenly paralyzed. He couldn't even blink. After the incident, the man realized that his stepmother had been saved by her absolute conviction in Kuan Yin, who had the power to protect all beings, no matter how malicious. He also realized that, although he had had no faith in Kuan Yin at the time, she had saved him from the sin of murder. He became her devotee. The stepmother, for her part, stopped being cruel from that point on and became a much kinder person.

So it is clear that we need to grow in trust and devotion. The Outer Buddha Stage builds that foundation. The remaining three Buddha Stages increasingly deepen devotion and trust until we awaken to our fullest human potential—realizing the absolute nature.

The benefits we receive from the Four Stages of meditation are commensurate with our level of trust and devotion. Having no devotion or trust doesn't mean that the Buddha's blessings are not with us. It just means that we are not receptive to him and have a hard time acknowledging and receiving his blessings. The Buddha said:

> In the minds of people who have no trust
> Virtuous Dharma will not take place—
> Like green shoots from burnt seeds.[66]

We are propelled on the path by the fervor of our devotion. It causes our mind to blossom boundlessly and our body to fill with blissful heat. We feel compelled to devote every aspect of our mind to the Buddha. Our longing to commune with him pushes us to awaken to the unity of our mind with his, and to realize the true nature of our own mind and the ultimate pure nature of all, which is enlightenment. The more we see his enlightened qualities, the stronger our devotion and trust, and the more quickly we arrive at our ultimate goal, enlightenment.

4

THE ESSENCE OF
LOVING-KINDNESS

LOVING-KINDNESS IS THE ESSENCE and nature of the whole world and of every being. To see and experience this is to realize who we are. We can all observe that, if someone is in a quiet, undisturbed place—for example, in nature— he or she will become more peaceful. The more peaceful that person becomes, the more joyful, wise, and helpful they will be to others. That is a clue that our human nature in its normal, undisturbed state is not violent or harmful, but loving.

If we could reach and express our own loving nature, we wouldn't merely be enjoying a wonderful state. We would be opening our heart and body, and the hearts and bodies of every receptive being, with the energy of the joy of loving-kindness. All of our expressions would become a source of illumination of peace and joy to the world.

In the same way that olive oil is the essence of the olive fruit, loving-kindness is the heart of human purity. So to awaken our own loving-kindness and offer such a great feast to all is the true potential and meaning of every being.

However, although a loving heart is our birthright, it won't necessarily shine forth suddenly unless we make an effort. It unfortunately becomes a stranger when we become submerged in our daily struggles and emotions. So we need to work hard to uncover it through meditation and mental and physical dedication.

It is one of the many paradoxes of spiritual life that generating loving-kindness toward others is one of the fastest ways to make ourselves happy. The Buddha said:

> If you meditate on loving-kindness
> And love all kin and friends
> And all the forces of the elements,
> Your happiness will greatly increase.[67]

With loving-kindness, we become joyful and make many merits—the positive effects of the practice of virtuous thoughts and deeds, which become the seeds of future happiness. The Buddha said:

> If you meditate on compassion and loving-kindness
> Toward relatives, friends, and spirit beings,
> The experience of joy greatly increases in you.
> If you don't harbor any hatred for any being,
> But only [have] loving-kindness, then your deeds
> become virtuous.
> If you have compassion in your mind toward all
> beings
> You will generate great merits as the Noble Ones
> did.[68]

But meditating on loving-kindness does so much more. It leads us to the highest states of realization, for loving-kindness is at the heart of high meditations such as "emptiness," which is the unbounded, nondual, and fully awakened state of openness. The more we train ourselves to wish joy for others, the more we loosen the tightening rope of our mind's grasping at "self" and selfish attitudes. As that happens, our negative emotions, like attachment and hatred, will subside. And the walls that we habitually erect between self and other, between "us" and "them," between this and that, will erode, bringing us closer and closer to the true nature that we all share.

The true realization of emptiness entails realizing emptiness with the essence of compassion and loving-kindness. The Third Dodrupchen explains:

> Compassion with the essence of emptiness means compassion that is free from concepts.[69]

Aspiration and Practice: The Two Levels of Generating Loving-Kindness

Bodhichitta is the heart of both the path and goal of Mahayana Buddhism. Loving-kindness—wishing joy and enlightenment for all—is an integral part of that bodhichitta. There are two stages of bodhichitta: absolute bodhichitta, which is beyond concepts, and relative bodhichitta, where we still have concepts. In order to realize absolute bodhichitta, we need to practice relative bodhichitta.

There are two levels of relative bodhichitta: aspirational and engaged. Aspirational bodhichitta is about cultivating the wish, the deep desire, that all beings be happy and enlightened. Engaged bodhichitta is about putting that aspiration into practice by serving others practically, physically, verbally, and spiritually. This can include giving alms, making offerings, and teaching Dharma as well as engaging in meditations and prayers on loving-kindness, devotion, and wisdom for the sake of others. Shantideva writes:

Bodhichitta can be condensed into two:
The "aspirational" aspect of bodhichitta and
The "engaged" aspect of bodhichitta.
The difference is like that between wishing to travel
    and actually traveling.[70]

Shantideva beautifully explains the merits of these two aspects of bodhichitta:

The bodhichitta of aspiration
Produces great fruits while living in the world,
But not as much as engaged bodhichitta does,
Which produces merits unceasingly. When you have
    developed
[Engaged] bodhichitta
For liberating infinite beings
In your mind irreversibly,
From then on, even if you are sleeping or careless,
The stream of merits progresses ceaselessly
To the extent of space. . . .
If even the mere thought of benefiting a person
Is superior to making offerings to the Buddha,
Then there can be no question about
Striving to benefit all beings without remainder. . . .

While other virtuous deeds are like plantain trees—
Which perish after bearing fruit—
Bodhichitta always
Expands after bearing fruits. . . .
If they develop bodhichitta,
From that moment, the very beings fettered in
    samsara
Will become known as the children of the Buddha.[71]

Suggesting how important it is to develop bodhichitta, Patrul Rinpoche makes earnest aspirations for it:

If you have bodhichitta, that is all you need for
    attaining Buddhahood.
If you don't have it, you can't attain enlightenment.
May I develop the unmistaken seed of attaining
    Buddhahood—
Pure bodhichitta.
May bodhichitta progress higher and higher.
May I never forget bodhichitta in my successive lives.
May I train in the activities of the bodhisattvas
By meditating on bodhichitta again and again.[72]

Infinite Beings Have Been Our Mothers in Our Past Lives

In the beginning, it can sometimes be hard to open our warm hearts even to some of our loved ones, let alone strangers. But if we don't have that warmheartedness, we won't be able to really help them or even have a genuine smile on our face. The important thing, according to the teachings, is to remember that those we meet are not, in fact, strangers. Our encounters with "unknown" people are not coincidental. They are all the very closely connected loved ones of our past.

Buddhism teaches that every single being in the universe, down to the tiniest insect, was our loving mother in our past lives. The number of these mother-beings is without measure. The Buddha said:

As limitless as the extent of space,
So are beings limitless.[73]

When these so-called strangers were our mother, they gave birth to us and cared for us as their beloved child with unconditional love, making great sacrifices for us, as a mother bird does with her little ones, watching over, feeding, and protecting them even at the cost of her own life. Each being has loved us this way. So we owe them a huge debt of gratitude, and must meditate on feeling and recognizing every being as our present loving mother.

Every mother-being wants to be happy, just as a thirst-tormented person wants water. Most beings, however, have no idea how to secure happiness. Confused, they grasp at anything that they think will be rewarding. But they go about it in the wrong way—through grasping, attachment, obsession, or aggression. At best, they are chasing rainbows. At worst, they end up hurting themselves, like someone who tries to lick honey off the sharp edge of a knife.

Since, fortunately, we are on the right path in this life and understand the true causes of happiness, we owe it to all our dear mother-beings to joyfully take responsibility for bringing them everlasting happiness and Buddhahood without leaving anyone behind. As Pandita Padma Wangchen[74] says:

> Then we must practice what causes benefits and happiness [for all].[75]

We must be ready to forge ahead on their behalf and bear any hardship or lack of gratitude that we may encounter.

If we could extend loving-kindness to all infinite mother-beings in the universe, we would have inconceivably vast loving-kindness and create immeasurable merits. The Buddha said:

> The realm of beings is boundless. It is inexhaustible. So, too, the loving-kindness meditation of the bodhisattvas is boundless. It is inexhaustible. Since beings are as limitless as space, therefore the loving-kindness of those superior beings [bodhisattvas] is inexhaustible.[76]

Wishing for Beings' Happiness Alone versus Wishing for Both Their Happiness and Their Enlightenment

There is a difference between wishing our mother-beings happiness alone, and wishing them *both* happiness *and* full enlightenment. The former is called a "virtuous attitude."[77] Training in it will bring us happiness and rebirth in celestial realms. By itself, however, that won't lead to the attainment of liberation or Buddhahood. The reason is that it lacks thoughts of renunciation, the development of bodhichitta, the realization of the view of emptiness, and realization of the absence of "self."

By contrast, wishing others *both* happiness *and* full enlightenment is called a "boundless attitude."[78] This is loving-kindness, one of "four boundless attitudes" that Mahayana Buddhism urges us to train in. The other three are compassion (the wish that no one should suffer or be separated from joy); sympathetic joy (rejoicing in the happiness of others); and equanimity (wishing well toward all beings equally). Training in loving-kindness as a boundless attitude leads to the development of bodhichitta, which in turn leads to Buddhahood.

As Patrul Rinpoche writes:

> The four boundless attitudes are the unmistaken causes of developing bodhichitta.[79]

Importantly, if we develop boundless loving-kindness, then the other three boundless attitudes will easily germinate in our mind.

Explaining the distinction between "living a pious life" (developing the four virtuous attitudes) and nurturing boundless attitudes, Longchen Rabjam writes:

> If they [the trainings] are not integrated with the path of liberation from samsara,
> Then they are called the four ways of "living a pious life" that cause [rebirth in] samsara.
> If they are integrated with the path of peace [enlightenment],

Then they are called "the four boundless [attitudes]"
    that will take one beyond the ocean of samsara.[80]

This distinction between wishing only happiness and
wishing both happiness and enlightenment is made in the
sutras as well. One sutra says:

> The four aspirations, such as loving-kindness, that
> are not integrated with bodhichitta cause only
> worldly happiness. They are called the "four ways
> of living a pious life" [four virtuous attitudes]. The
> four aspirations that are integrated with bodhi-
> chitta cause nirvana. They are called the "four
> boundless attitudes."[81]

So whatever Dharma practice we do, we should do
with the four boundless attitudes—with the aspiration for
all beings to attain happiness *and* enlightenment.

We can never be too advanced to practice the four
boundless attitudes. As beginners, we practice them in order to learn how to generate them. As more advanced students, we practice them in order to strengthen them. We
should study important works on them, such as *Tsemezhi
Gyacher Drelwa* (The Explanation of the Four Boundless
Attitudes) by Buddhagupta.[82]

All this might sound complex, but according to great
meditation Masters, the four boundless attitudes can be
condensed into simply having good thoughts and a good
attitude.[83]

So, thinking about our infinite mother-beings who are
deprived of happiness and enlightenment, we should wish:

"May all mother-beings enjoy happiness and the causes of happiness for the time being, and may they all ultimately attain full enlightenment, the supreme happiness. I will dedicate my life to bringing them happiness and enlightenment." Or we could wish: "May I attain enlightenment so that I can bring happiness and enlightenment to all mother-beings through my enlightened power." We could also say this popular Tibetan Buddhist prayer, which captures the aspirations of the four boundless attitudes:

> May all beings enjoy happiness and the causes of happiness.
> May they be free from suffering and the causes of suffering.
> May they never be separated from the supreme happiness that is free from suffering.
> May they remain in the mind of boundless equanimity free from both attachment to kin and hatred of foes.[84]

After generating such aspirations, we must put that wish into practice by pursuing spiritual trainings and serving others' needs with complete commitment. This training embodies the development of both loving-kindness and bodhichitta. Maitreya-natha says:

> Bodhichitta is the development of the wish to attain full enlightenment
> For the benefit of others.[85]

The Third Dodrupchen writes:

The meaning of developing bodhichitta in one's mind is developing the uncontrived wish to attain Buddhahood for the sake of all beings.[86]

There are successively higher stages of loving-kindness attainments that can be reached. Beginners can attain levels of loving-kindness consistent with the path of accumulation and the path of application (the first two of the "five paths"). This involves developing loving-kindness by seeing every being as our mother.

More advanced meditators can reach levels of loving-kindness that accord with the first through seventh stages of the tenfold bodhisattva path. This entails developing loving-kindness with reference to the nature of phenomena,[87] by wishing that all beings who haven't yet realized the nature of phenomena, realize it.

Even more advanced students can attain levels of loving-kindness consistent with the three pure stages—that is, the eighth, ninth, and tenth stages of the Tenfold Bodhisattva Stages. The practice here is in loving-kindness free from concepts. This is the ultimate (or absolute) bodhichitta[88] free from elaborations.[89] It is the training in the spontaneously accomplished loving-kindness free from thoughts.

The First Dodrupchen[90] describes these three levels of attainment of loving-kindness:

> Knowing that all the beings of higher and lower realms [of samsara] have been one's father and mother, and wishing them not to have even the slightest experience of hurt or violence, as a child

[wishes] for his or her mother, is the thought of loving-kindness that focuses on beings.

The bodhisattvas who attained the first stage up to the seventh stage are helping beings who are suffering [as the result of their] attachment to phenomena by perceiving them as real, though they have no reality—through teachings that will help them to realize the true nature of phenomena.

That is the loving-kindness focused on phenomena. [Bodhisattvas who have attained] the eighth stage or higher enjoy the loving-kindness that is free from concepts. Like wish-fulfilling gems, the loving-kindness of the Victorious Ones[91] spontaneously serves the world because of their past aspirations, even though they are free from concepts.[92]

A sutra says:

"What are the three loving-kindnesses? They are the loving-kindness that focuses on beings, the loving-kindness that focuses on phenomena, and the loving-kindness free from concepts."[93]

Whatever Dharma training we are pursuing—say, generosity—we should do it with emptiness united with loving-kindness if we can. The Third Dodrupchen writes:

You must train in giving with emptiness that is with the essence of compassion.[94]

However, right now, meditating on these various higher stages of loving-kindness may be hard for many of us to even comprehend, let alone practice. Though it is good if we understand and are interested in them, the important thing is to start from where we are.

So, whenever we can, we should exert ourselves to strengthen our loving-kindness. We should build the power of our confidence in the Buddha's loving-kindness, in our receiving his blessings, and in our own mind. We should make our aspirations ever-broader and more inconceivable, and inclusive of all infinite beings. As Nagarjuna[95] writes:

> As the phenomena of beings are infinite,
> So, too, does the wish of joy [for them] become infinite.[96]

We should enhance the purity of our goals, making them ever more selfless to the point that we have the "measureless loving-kindness." Je Gampopa says:

> You must try to develop a true wish of having happiness and benefit for all beings, limitless as space. If such a wish is developed—that is the actual loving-kindness. . . . Because of the force of kindness, if your eyes well up with tears and the hairs on your body stand up—that is the great loving-kindness. If you could develop this wish equally toward all beings—that is the measureless loving-kindness.[97]

What Great Masters Say about Loving-Kindness

Meditations on loving-kindness have been taught and praised by some of the greatest scholars of the four major Buddhist schools of Tibet. I summarize them here because each of these scholars understood and embodied Buddhist meditations on loving-kindness, and each presents his insights in a slightly different way. It is important that we follow them accordingly.

Je Gampopa Sönam Rinchen (1079–1153) of the Kagyu school writes:

> Division: There are three divisions. They are: doing loving-kindness meditation on beings, doing loving-kindness meditation on phenomena, and doing loving-kindness meditation that is free from concepts. The *Lodrö Mizepe Tenpa* sutra explains:

> "Loving-kindness of thinking about beings is the meditation of the bodhisattvas who have just developed bodhichitta. Loving-kindness of thinking about phenomena is the meditation of the bodhisattvas who are engaged in [bodhisattvas'] activities. Loving-kindness that is free from concepts is the meditation of the bodhisattvas who have attained confidence in the unborn truth."[98]

> Here, I will discuss the first one. In this, the object of meditation is all beings. The way of doing meditation is wishing them to have happiness. The formula of meditation: the root is remembering the

kindnesses, so you must remember the kindness of beings. In this life, the kindest person for you is your own mother. What sort of kindness has she shown you? There are four: the kindness of developing your body, dealing with hardships [for you], giving you your life, and showing you the world. ... As her kindness is infinite for you, you must develop loving-kindness, the thought of wishing her happiness, from your heart. Then not only her, but to all beings who have been your mother. Whoever has been your mother has been as kind to you as your [present] mother is. ... So you must meditate to develop a genuine thought of wishing to help all beings and wishing happiness for all beings, limitless as the extent of space. When such thought is developed in your mind, that is the real loving-kindness. ... Then, because of the power of this feeling of loving-kindness, tears will come to your eyes and your body's hairs will stand up. That is the development of the great loving-kindness. When you have such experiences equally toward all beings, that will be [the development of] immeasurable loving-kindness. When you have no wish to have happiness for yourself, but only for others, then you will have perfected loving-kindness.[99]

Pandita Kunga Gyaltshen (1182–1251) of the Sakya School writes about loving-kindness:

How to meditate: It will be easier to meditate if you see all beings as your loved ones. In some sutras, it is taught to meditate on them as your mothers. Some tantras, such as *Dorje Tsemo*,[100] teach you to see beings as your child. There is no person who hasn't been your father, brother, and so on. So you must train to meditate on loving-kindness toward all beings [by seeing them] as the person you feel close to and care for.

However, wishing that sentient beings be happy alone is not enough. You need to meditate from your heart-core, wishing that all beings have not just happiness but also the causes of happiness. Happiness means being joyful as the result of mentally and physically living in accordance with Dharma. Wishing to have the cause of happiness means [wishing them] to meet holy Dharma, since if you train in Dharma, the cause, you will have ultimate joy as the result. By familiarizing yourself with these again and again, loving-kindness toward all beings as a mother toward her only child will take birth.[101]

Omniscient Longchen Rabjam (1308–1363) of the Nyingma school writes:

The object of meditation of loving-kindness is all beings.
The method is to meditate on wishing that one
　　person, [building up to] all,
In all directions to the limits [of space],
Enjoy the temporary happiness of the gods and
　　human realms

And the ultimate happiness, enlightenment.
The sign [of your progress] is that the excellent
    universal loving-kindness,
A love that is greater than that of a mother for her
    only child,
Will take place.
At the end, contemplate the state of equanimity,
The great loving-kindness that is free from concepts.
The sign [of perfection] is unifying loving-kindness
    and emptiness.
The result is that you will see [beings] to be pleasing
    and pure.[102]

Je Tsongkhapa Lobzang Tragpa (1357–1419), founder of the Gelug school, writes:

Pay attention to beings who are bereft of happiness. The method is thinking, "How wonderful if they were happy!" "May they all have happiness." "I will provide them with happiness." . . . The sequence of doing meditation on loving-kindness is: First meditate on loved ones. Then gradually meditate on neutral beings, then on foes, and then on all beings. The ways of doing meditation are [as follows]: You must think again and again about the suffering that beings endure. Then compassion will develop in you. Likewise, you must think about how beings are bereft of happiness—both contaminated and uncontaminated happiness.[103] When you really feel this, then you will spontaneously wish them happiness. Then think about various kinds of happiness in your mind and offer them to those beings.[104]

5

THE FOUR BUDDHA STAGES

THE MEDITATIONS IN THIS BOOK help us steadily increase our loving-kindness, bodhichitta. We start with the first stage, the Outer Buddha, because, in my experience, it is easier to develop loving-kindness by first developing devotion and trust in the Buddha and by feeling and receiving his loving-kindness. The Buddha said:

> When you remember Lord Avalokiteshvara,
> Your mind instantly becomes the mind of loving-
> kindness.[105]

In the second stage, the Inner Buddha, we recognize the loving-kindness that the Buddha has activated in our own mind and contemplate it. We then expand that feeling of loving-kindness to the entire universe.

If we practice with that state of mind, we will benefit all receptive beings in their present life and cause them happiness and enlightenment in their future lives.

Actually, because we become what we think, our mind already becomes a mind of loving-kindness in the first stage, since we think about and feel the Buddha's loving-kindness then. In the second stage, however, we start to see and enjoy the Buddha's loving-kindness as awakened in our own mindstream, in our own heart and body. The unconditional love that we saw and felt in the first stage, we now understand as being within us. In the second stage, the epicenter of the theater of our spiritual experience is our own mind, instead of somewhere external "out there."

At first, our awakening might be fleeting. However, no matter how long it lasts, it is important that we recognize that the Buddha's loving-kindness is not somewhere else. It is present in us. Our newfound inner loving-kindness has actually always been there as our own true inherent pure quality, as Buddhism teaches. But we need to discover and realize it, which we do through the meditations in the second stage. We must keep enjoying and rejoicing in the discovery of the great awakening of loving-kindness within us. By remaining and resting in it over and over again, we strengthen it so that it becomes a long-lasting state.

As always, we must guard against falling into the trap of letting our ego swell, thinking "I am pretty good" or "I'm a realized one," and against burning with attachment to "me," "mine," or "my" meditative experience. Nor should we allow ourselves to collapse due to lack of self-confidence, thinking, "My experiences can't be real" or "I'm not good enough."

The key is to keep doing whatever meditation we are doing, without fear or hope, doubts or expectations, because these are the two major issues for meditators until they transcend all obstructions.

Keep Connected with the Outer Buddha

Whatever progress we make, we must keep connected with the Outer Buddha. That will strengthen our fledgling new feelings of loving-kindness. When we feel the Outer Buddha's loving presence, it is almost impossible not to develop the blissful heat of trust and devotion to him.

The feeling of devotional bliss arouses an uncontrived and spontaneous trust in the Buddha. Every hair of our body will start to rise and tears of joy will start to rain from our eyes. These are the indications that the true blessings of the Buddha of Loving-Kindness have entered our mindstream and true spiritual attainments of loving-kindness have taken birth in us. Our heart's mundane thoughts and emotions will transform into the energies and movements of enlightened qualities. If we could keep remembering the Outer Buddha and his loving-kindness and could experience that newfound unconditional love within us, even the hardest-hearted of us would transform into beings with flower-like minds that are soft, gentle, radiant, and loving.

So we need not only to realize that loving-kindness has developed within us, but also to maintain and nurture that realization through the skillful means of meditation with vibrant memories of our meditative experiences and consistent mindfulness. The more vividly we can see the Buddha's loving face, filled with his beautiful, joyful smile, the more strongly we can feel his unconditional love in our heart. And the more we can maintain that state, the more firmly the experience of loving-kindness will be anchored in our heart and the more stable, perfect, and pure our progress will be.

Remain in the Newborn Loving-Kindness of the Mind

Again and again, we must enjoy and remain in the newborn loving-kindness of our mind. We must rejoice and celebrate over the new dawn without grasping. We must rejoice over and over again at the awakening of such a precious treasure in us. By pouring in the energy of rejoicing and celebrating, we strengthen the power of our loving-kindness and greatly extend and deepen its scope.

We should prolong and expand thoughts and feelings of loving-kindness for all and try to integrate it into our every mental and physical activity—instead of falling into waves of turbulent thoughts, emotions, and actions. Pray again and again, "May this amazing loving-kindness, bodhichitta, be fully developed in my mind and in the mind of every mother-being." This is the focal point of our training in loving-kindness.

Dealing with Various Obstacles

The obstacles that we may face include having expectations, lack of self-confidence, indifference, and unwholesome distractions and activities. If we keep entertaining these negative acts and not believing in ourselves, thinking, "I'm not doing the practice well enough," "I'm not capable," "Everything is fated, so why should I try?"—at best, these acts and thoughts will divert us from our goal and slow down our spiritual progress. At worst, indulging in distractions, unwholesome activities, and negative attitudes will drag us on the wrong track and slowly lead us into the worst possible way of living, destroying all the possible fruits that this amazing human life could bring us.

It is important for us to reflect on how we got to where we are today and how we can change in the future. Let me illustrate how our thoughts and feelings can change the quality and direction of our life. Unfortunately, if I use a negative story, it might be easier for us to get the point, as we are all personally well versed in such things.

So, say that we have an unpleasant exchange with a co-worker one day. It isn't significant, but we keep thinking about it and feeling dislike for that person. Soon, whatever this person says or does, whether it actually touches us or not, annoys us. Every exchange, whether smiling or frowning, triggers harsh feelings in us toward them. After some time, even seeing this person's e-mail in our inbox can make our heart skip a beat. Then, merely thinking about this person makes us feel frustrated and miserable. It doesn't matter if they are miles away. It consumes us. We constantly bring their annoying demeanor vividly to mind and keep hearing their irritating voice loudly—as if they were right in our face. Obviously, real harmful actions and harsh words will fly back and forth when you actually meet. We may force ourselves to smile, but whatever we say or do relating to this person will become harmful. Our forced nice gestures won't charm anyone, as they came from an agitated state of mind. This illustration is probably familiar to many of us.

But it is ourselves that we harm most. We accumulate poisonous emotions that hurt the elements and energy systems of our body and can lead to sickness and disease.

So this means that we can lead our lives in the right direction by controlling our mental attitude. We should learn to refrain from falling into the misery dumps of life by moving forward with our positive mental and emotional experiences, such as our meditations on loving-kindness.

At the same time, we must also refrain from grasping at our meditation experiences, getting attached to them, craving the feeling of loving-kindness, or constantly looking for other new paths. Just enjoy the qualities of your newfound experience with full attentiveness and remain in it as if you were resting in your own cozy, familiar home, with total ease, freedom, and openness.

We must have confidence that, by the power of focusing our mind on the Buddha of Loving-Kindness with devotion, the total openness, loving-kindness, which has always been ready to awaken in our mind, has now been awakened. With such unwavering confidence, we should recognize and trust that loving-kindness has taken birth in us today!

Our Karma Determines Our Future

According to Buddhism, the cycles of cause and effect of our negative deeds (karma) yield only pain. When we die and our mind escapes from the web of our material body, we begin our journey through the transitional state (*bardo*) to our next rebirth. Whether our subsequent rebirths are pleasant or not depends on the habits that we have generated in our mind. Whatever negative experience we have today is the product of some unwholesome mental and emotional tendency, or karma, from our past. In the earlier example, the unhappy episode grew from a thought of disliking a co-worker.

Karma can also work in our favor, however. Thanks to karma, if we could sow a seed of positive perceptions and feelings, we could turn our mental and emotional tendencies to positive ones and start to enjoy a peaceful and joyful life.

That's why, if we can see clearly and feel deeply the incredible qualities of the Buddha of Loving-Kindness from our hearts, and if we can strengthen that feeling, then before long, our mind will be able to enjoy the Buddha's real enlightened qualities. His all-knowing wisdom, unconditional love, and invincible power will gradually awaken in us. Our mental and physical activities will turn into the sources of benefits for many, as we share the lights of love and happiness with whomever we are in communication with.

Reasons for Specific Visualizations

We can improve the qualities of our mind by changing how we perceive things. That's the reason we visualize the Buddha of Loving-Kindness in the form of light. Light softens the rigidity and harshness of our mind. It makes us soft and gentle. We see the Buddha as radiant and captivating in order to wake up from sleepiness, dullness, and indifference. Focusing on his various qualities gives us less scope to wander or indulge in unwholesome thoughts and introduces us to various enlightened qualities. We see his kind face and blossoming smile and feel his loving presence to turn our minds toward loving-kindness. We need an image that inspires us so that we will want to dedicate the precious hours of our life to training in virtuous qualities. Dwelling in loving-kindness purifies all our mental and emotional impurities. Receiving the blessings of his wisdom, love, and power awakens the enlightened wisdom, love, and power of our own mind.

Transforming Our Mind and Body in the Second Buddha Stage, the Inner Buddha

In the Second Buddha Stage, we work with transforming the body, using the breath, the sound of the mantra, and visualizations to fill it with waves of blissful heat of devotion and loving-kindness and turn every particle of it into particles of blessing light, light of wisdom, love, and power.

We additionally work with our surroundings, feeling that they are imbued with the energies of our loving-kindness—just as when the sun rises, the whole earth is pervaded by the sun's light and warmth.

But actually, although we are wholeheartedly serving others, these meditations have the greatest impact on our own mind, for when we are perceiving our surroundings as loving-kindness or our body with energy waves of loving-kindness, it is our mind that is generating and enjoying the meditation. So in the second stage, our body and environment become a source of loving-kindness via the mind.

Loving-Kindness in the Third Buddha Stage, the Universal Buddha

In the Third Buddha Stage, we meditate on whatever we see, hear, and feel as the images, sounds, and feelings of loving-kindness, possessing its qualities of natural radiance—just as when the sun shines, the whole world turns into the world of daylight.

When our mind is transformed into a mind filled with the qualities of loving-kindness, all appearances that our mind perceives will naturally arise as a world with the qualities of loving-kindness. Everything we see, hear, and feel is actually an appearance projected by our mind. So if our mind is filled with loving-kindness, appearances will reflect the pure qualities of that mind. We will see the whole universe in the qualities of the Buddha of Loving-Kindness and his Pure Land.

The Progression of Loving-Kindness

Importantly, however, as long as we are still at the beginning of our journey in Third Buddha Stage, our experiences of loving-kindness might still be just glimpses that are neither powerful nor everlasting, since our meditation is not yet perfected. We will still be seeing and feeling phenomena in ordinary forms, such as earthly houses or the sounds of roaring traffic, with tight subjective and objective duality. Beings will not yet appear or function for us as Buddhas of Loving-Kindness. And the world will not yet appear for us as the Pure Land. So although we feel loving-kindness, our experience at this early part of the Third Buddha Stage will simply be seeing, hearing, and feeling with the *qualities* of loving-kindness, rather than the *actual* Buddha presence or *actual* Buddha qualities. (That is why I speak of "qualities" of loving-kindness in a number of places.)

To encourage or inspire ourselves to further our meditation, instead of looking at how far we still have to go, we should look back at how far we've come and rejoice over that repeatedly. It's the same as when we are weary from traveling. We should rest and look toward where we came from, as that will cheer us up. Shantideva writes:

When you are resting,
Rest by facing back [toward where you came].[106]

When, as the result of vigorous continuous meditation, we reach higher levels of realization, then even ordinary beings might appear to us in the form of beings of love and wisdom, and the world may appear in the form of wisdom-light. We might even perceive them as the qualities of illusory appearances of wisdom, love, and power of the Buddha of Loving-Kindness in the state of nonduality.

It is unusual, however, to find people enjoying such high experiences, because meditators who have dedicated their lives deeply to practice are rare. Nevertheless, if we could enjoy even some limited qualities of loving-kindness in our heart, that will empower us to see the world as one of peace, joy, and love, and to serve others.

So, until we reach high stages of realization, we will still be perceiving all images dualistically in their ordinary forms as we did before—except now they will be refined and permeated by the peaceful, joyful qualities of loving-kindness. We will be able to perceive all images as sources for advancing our training in loving-kindness.

Likewise, we will still be hearing all sounds of nature and beings as ordinary sounds, as before—except now they will resound and be heard with virtuous qualities that inspire loving-kindness and the means of expressing it.

All our thoughts and feelings will still be arising in their ordinary way—dualistically and emotionally, as before—except now they will be permeated by positive perceptions and joyful experiences, the qualities of loving-kindness. So, even though we might not yet see everything as Buddha and Buddha Pure Land, the cycle of a peaceful and joyful life will have truly started to revolve.

If a trainee, a bodhisattva, has fully accomplished a meditation like loving-kindness or compassion, however, he or she will experience multiple spiritual attainments such as seeing all as the world of the Buddha of Loving-Kindness or as the Buddha's qualities, and will realize loving-kindness free from concepts. A sutra says:

Bodhisattva[107] Avalokiteshvara beseeched the Buddha: "O Blessed One, bodhisattvas should not train in many dharmas. If a bodhisattva takes one dharma and fully realizes it, O Blessed One, then all the dharmas of Buddhahood will be in his or her hand. What is that one dharma? It is the great compassion! O Blessed One, [by realizing] the great compassion, all the dharmas of the Buddha will be in that bodhisattva's palm."[108]

Rigdzin Godem[109] says:

Lights are projected from the body [of the Buddha] and
All forms become divine forms—the union of
    emptiness and appearances:

The Great Compassionate One, the King of the Noble
    Ones.
Lights are projected from the mantra [of the Buddha],
    and all sounds such as the sound of the elements
Become the sounds of mantra—the union of
    emptiness and sound.
Recollections and thoughts remain in the state of
    freedom from arising, abiding, and cessation, and
Rest in the realization that transcends all thoughts,
    expressions, and designations.[110]

Further, if we are pursuing meditations on realizing
the deities of compassion or loving-kindness as taught in
esoteric (tantric) training, then whatever we are seeing—
beings or nature—should arise as the deities and their
pure lands; whatever sounds we are hearing should arise
as the energy waves of mantras; and whatever thoughts
we are thinking should arise as the awareness wisdom, the
union of emptiness and loving-kindness. If we do this, our
spiritual attainments will progress through the five paths
and the ten stages.

Loving-Kindness in the Fourth Buddha Stage, the Ultimate Buddha

The focus here is on the perfection of the realized awareness of ultimate loving-kindness, the union of all—nondual and free from concepts.

    We attain the Ultimate Buddha as a result of ad-
vancing through and perfecting the meditations of the
Outer, Inner, and Universal Buddha. In the Fourth Stage,

all arises, or is realized, as one in the true nature of loving-kindness—loving-kindness that is free from concepts, duality, emotions, and sensations. In this state, we enjoy total confidence in what we are seeing and feeling—the absolute loving-kindness, the fully opened and totally awakened state with its enlightened energies. All are united in one nature and quality, the unstained and fully opened loving-kindness that encompasses all.

When we realize universal loving-kindness in the Third Buddha Stage, in order to elevate it to the final step, the Ultimate Buddha, we must dissolve all our mental concepts and emotional energies, positive or negative, and realize the fully opened awareness wisdom. We mustn't let our mind start running after past thoughts and sensations through the key of our memories. We mustn't let our minds bring in future dreams and ideas through the hook of our imagination. Nor must we let our mind grasp at present thoughts and sensations through our dualistic concepts and diehard habits. When we watch the present moment with the fully opened energy of loving-kindness without any trace of grasping—we will find no present thought that is standing anymore to hold on to, just as there is nothing to grasp on to in the sky, for the true nature of all is beyond existence.

If we can fully realize and maintain this meditation experience, then it will be possible for us to actually realize the true face of ultimate loving-kindness, as it is. That is called loving-kindness free from concepts. The true face or nature of loving-kindness does not exist in any form or character of this or that. It is free from conditions. It is beyond the four extremes—existence; non-existence;

neither existence nor non-existence; and both existence and non-existence. It is beyond the cyclic operation of the three spheres—subject, object, and actions of the mind. It is the union of awareness and emptiness; of wisdom and loving-kindness—freedom from elaborations. It is the meaning of suchness, the ultimate truth. It is the state of ultimate loving-kindness, Buddhahood. So we must let go of all conceptualities and rest in the intrinsic awareness, the experience of boundless loving-kindness, as it is. Rigdzin Godem writes:

> If one's mind remains free from grasping, without thinking or conceptualizing anything, then it has been introduced to the state of indivisibility from the mind of the Buddha.[111]

In order to perfect this realization in the highest state of ultimate loving-kindness, we must train ourselves to maintain that experience by remaining in it.

When the state of ultimate loving-kindness is perfected, all forms or images will appear and function for us as the Buddha of Loving-Kindness and his Pure Land, in the nature of the union of appearances and emptiness, the union of loving-kindness and wisdom, and the union of Buddha wisdom and Buddha Pure Land. They will appear in their boundless nature, untouched by mental, emotional, dualistic, or sensory traps. All appearances will arise as the indivisible, infinite, and boundless power of loving-kindness that is free from conceptual configurations. This is emptiness or openness, as it is fully open and unbounded by any concept.

Then all sounds will resound for us as the union of sound and emptiness—boundless sound that is free from concepts. All thoughts will arise in the nature of the union of loving-kindness and emptiness—without even a trace of dualistic apprehensions, emotional clashes, or sensory thirst. All details will be seen in the nature of a single great unity and absolute freedom, like the apparitions of infinite images in a mirror without limits or afflictions.

According to Buddhism, all existents abide in loving-kindness free from concepts in their absolute nature. But the understanding and realization of that true nature have been covered over by the webs of our own mental, emotional, and intellectual obscurations.

Now, in order to uncover the true nature and its qualities, we must dispel the covering—our unhealthy concepts, emotions, and actions. Through the power of devotion and contemplation, we must uncover and see the true innate enlightened qualities—loving-kindness that is free from concepts—shining forever. Then all arisings will awaken and function as the Buddha and Buddha Pure Land forever.

Two Wings of the Bird: The Two Accumulations

By training in the Four Buddha Stages, we attain Buddhahood by perfecting the two accumulations: (1) creating merits and (2) realizing wisdom. According to Mahayana Buddhism, meditating on such qualities as devotion and loving-kindness, saying prayers, and serving others are ways to accumulate merits, also known as "skillful means." Realizing the absolute wisdom, emptiness, and loving-kindness that is free from concepts is the way to accumulate wisdom. The perfection of these two accumulations is the attainment of Buddhahood.

Importantly, if all we do is stop our thoughts without having accomplished skillful means, we will not realize the wisdom that is the awakening of the true Buddha-nature of all.

So in order to liberate ourselves from samsaric bondage and realize ever-blossoming Buddhahood, we need to perfect the two accumulations. The two accumulations are like the wings of a bird. Both are needed for it to fly to its destiny. One without the other cannot free us from samsara, where we are currently trapped. That is why a sutra says:

> [Discriminative] wisdom that is not integrated
> with skillful means is bondage; but wisdom that
> is integrated with skillful means is liberation.
> Skillful means that is not integrated with wisdom
> is bondage; but skillful means that is integrated
> with wisdom is liberation.[112]

PART TWO

PRACTICE

*Meditations on
Loving-Kindness*

6

MEDITATION ON THE
OUTER BUDDHA

WE NOW TURN TO HOW to do the meditations, starting
with the Outer Buddha.

Preparation
SIT ON A COMFORTABLE SEAT, RELAX, AND BREATHE

Find a comfortable seat in a solitary or quiet place, and sit
in the Sevenfold Vairochana Posture (see Glossary) or the
half lotus posture. If this isn't comfortable, you can sit on
a chair or, if necessary, lie down. Whatever the position,
try to keep your spine straight if possible. If your back is
straight, your channels, arteries, and veins will be straight.
If your channels are straight, your breathing—or energy
waves—will be natural, with no blockages. When your
energy waves are tamed, they will naturally support the
mind's ability to engage in analytical or contemplative
meditations, as you desire.

If you feel any physical, mental, or spiritual dead energies, expel them through breathing exercises. That way,
your mind and body can function harmoniously without
stress or strain. You could use a simpler version of ninefold
breathing exercises for purifying and healing:

- Cycle one: Pressing your left index finger against your left nostril, exhale forcefully through your right nostril, thinking that all your sickness and karmas associated with fear and attachment are expelled fully in the form of a dark yellowish color. Repeat this two more times.
- Cycle two: Then, pressing your right index finger against your right nostril, exhale forcefully from your left nostril, visualizing and feeling that all your sickness and karmas associated with anger and hatred are fully expelled in the form of a dark reddish color from your body. Repeat this two more times.
- Cycle three: Then exhale three times through both nostrils simultaneously. While exhaling, see and feel that all your ills and karmas associated with confusion and ignorance are fully expelled in the form of darkness. Repeat this two more times.

Form the Right Intention: Bodhichitta

As you are getting ready to begin, make a commitment from the depth of your heart, thinking: "I am going to train myself in developing the precious bodhichitta, and pursue the ocean of trainings of the bodhisattva path such as loving-kindness and the Six Perfections, so that all my mother-beings will enjoy happiness for the time being, and ultimately attain Buddhahood." This way, you won't be meditating just for yourself, but you'll be earnestly embarking on the practice of limitlessly offering yourself to the service of all infinite beings.

Visualization

In this meditation, we will be visualizing the Buddha. Visualization is a powerful tool to focus and discipline the mind. The more clearly we can visualize an image and the longer we can hold it in our mind's eye, the greater our ability to concentrate on the meditation with firmness, calmness, and clarity. (See the color illustrations opposite pages 112 and 113 as an aid to visualization.)

In reality, we spend much of our time visualizing in our daily life. Most of our thoughts start with images that we engage with. If we could visualize positive images like the Buddha, that would inspire us to fully open and deeply feel his enlightening qualities and loving-kindness, and receive the blessings of his wisdom, love, and power. So, carefully and gently, we must start to build our skill in visualizing for the purpose of meditation.

The Sky, Flower, and Moon Cushion

Now, in the space before you, visualize a very clear, open, and beautiful sky. The sky is deep bright blue, as radiant as if it were made of rainbow light. This amazingly deep blue sky is brilliantly visible before your eyes, but free from any gross substance, as it is boundless empty space. It is vast, with no conceivable end or depth. It is naturally clean, clear, and bright, unpolluted by clouds or smoke. This boundless space is an immeasurable sphere that makes it possible for all beings to live, move, and function. It provides for the earth, nature, and all the materials of the universe.

With a relaxed mind, see and feel the sky's positive

qualities—its boundless openness, limitless freedom, immaculate purity, and luminous radiance from its depth—again and again.

When you see and enjoy the various amazing qualities of the sky, your mind starts feeling and becoming clear, radiant, boundless, and open, just like the sky. So, for a while, keep enjoying, opening to, and resting in the qualities of the sky—in your mind, heart, and body.

Then, in the center of that boundless, vast, clear sky, visualize a giant flower with billions and trillions of blossoming petals. Every part of the flower is made of intangible, colorful, radiant, brilliant light. The flower is as vast as a mountain and shines like the sun and moon. It emits and fills the space with a sweet fragrance. Keep enjoying the flower's blossoming qualities for a while.

Then, on top of this vast flower, visualize a moon cushion. It is clear and white like the moon that appears in the sky. It is a cushion made of white light—bright, shining, calm, cool, and clear.

Think about the beautiful details of the vast flower with a moon cushion on it in the boundless clear sky. Repeatedly enjoy their healthy qualities deeply and fully. These images, thoughts, and feelings help change the qualities of your mind slowly but surely to reflect the boundlessness, radiance, and openness that your mind has been perceiving.

THE BODY OF THE BUDDHA OF LOVING-KINDNESS

Now, in the middle of this vast sky as the background, atop this beautiful flower and moon cushion, visualize the Buddha of Loving-Kindness.

The body of the Buddha of Loving-Kindness is made of rainbow-like beautiful pure light. His body is the natural presence of his wisdom-light. His wisdom-light appears in various forms and qualities to fulfill the needs of all beings. His body is inseparable from his enlightened wisdom.

The Buddha's body is not a dualistic object with a gross form. Instead, he remains in the nature of self-radiant wisdom and wisdom-light. He is the ever-present body of loving-kindness and compassion—appearing luminously, resounding eloquently, and knowing all boundlessly. However, for beginners it is easier to try to visualize his form with details, each of which symbolizes various enlightened qualities. Buddhists use these symbols to generate devotion and understanding, as focal points of contemplation, objects of prayer and meditation, and sources of blessings.

Symbolizing that he is untouched by ordinary mental, emotional, and physical stains, and embodies infinite enlightened pure virtues, the complexion of the Buddha's body is immaculately white,[113] shining in all directions and glowing with enlightened radiance. His body shines as brightly as a snow mountain illuminated by the lights of a hundred thousand suns simultaneously. At the same time, his brightness is totally soothing to our mind's eye, like the healing light of a full moon.

His exceedingly beautiful body never tires, watching us continually. His appearance makes even the most beautiful celestial beings look dull by comparison.

His body has the nine peaceful qualities of peaceful Buddhas, being pliant, robust, delicate, flexible, youthful, clear, radiant, attractive, and captivating.

The Buddha's body is not made of gross substances

like flesh, blood, or earth, but of wisdom-light—light that is inseparable from his wisdom of enlightenment. He looks ever-youthful, like a sixteen-year-old, for he is free from aging or changing. His body is adorned with the thirty-two major marks and eighty minor signs[114] of a supreme Buddha—indications that he has perfected the dual accumulations. He is dressed in the thirteen ornamental costumes[115] of the Sambhogakaya, symbolizing that he is prosperous, possessing excellent enlightened qualities.

The Buddha's joyful, smiling face is beautiful like a blossoming white lotus in the sunlight. With his inconceivable loving-kindness, all beings can't help but find him unimaginably captivating. His loving eyes are always looking deeply and directly at each of you without blinking, indicating that his unconditional love for you is ceaseless—he doesn't even take the time to blink.

As the sign that he remains firmly in the state of the ultimate nature free from elaboration, the ultimate sphere of great peace, he sits on a lotus and moon seat in the firm vajra posture. Always keen to fulfill all the wishes of all beings with great loving-kindness, he holds at the level of his heart, between the palms of his first two hands, a wish-fulfilling gem glowing with light. The joining of his two palms symbolizes the indivisibility of samsara and nirvana or of emptiness and compassion.[116] The unending circle of the crystal mala that he holds in his right second hand represents the ceaseless nature of his loving enlightened activities for all beings. Indicating that he sees every detail of all things "as they are" and sees their true nature "as it is" with his omniscient wisdom, without any stain of dualistic concepts or afflicting emotions, he holds an immaculate white lotus with eight petals in his left second hand.

In the sky above his head as his "crown lord" sits the Buddha of Infinite Light (Amitabha) on a lotus and moon cushion amid an inconceivable expanse of beams, tents, nets, and rays of colorful lights, symbolizing that the Buddha of Loving-Kindness belongs to the Lotus Family (one of the five Buddha families).

This particular image described above—sitting with four arms—is the most widely used form of the Buddha of Loving-Kindness for meditation in Tibetan Buddhism, so I follow it here. However, the Buddha of Loving-Kindness has many other forms and colors that Tibetan Buddhists also meditate on.

For example, the Buddha of Loving-Kindness could be in a peaceful form, with two arms. He has a body of luminous light, symbolizing his purity. He is as youthful as a sixteen-year-old, symbolizing that he has transcended aging and change. He is attired in rich silk clothes and is adorned with precious jewels, symbolizing that he is endowed with the wealth of infinite Buddha qualities. He stands, indicating that he is always ready to serve others without resting. His right hand stretches down toward us in the gesture of "supreme giving," with a stream of nectar pouring from his palm to purify all our impurities, heal all our ills, and fulfill all our wishes. His left hand holds by the stem a blossoming white flower with a jewel at the center to symbolize that he is the union of loving-kindness and omniscient wisdom.

The other peaceful forms of the Buddha of Loving-Kindness include a standing Buddha with one head and four arms; a standing Buddha with eleven heads and four arms; and a standing Buddha with eleven heads and one thousand hands, with an eye in each palm.

The Buddha of Loving-Kindness also has a wrathful form, named Hayagriva. He is red and in a crouching pose, with two or more arms and a green neighing horse's head protruding from his head.

Buddhas manifest in wrathful forms to avert, tame, subdue, or eliminate harmful forces through the power of their wrathful expressions. Such expressions uniformly originate from loving-kindness, wisdom, and peace for the purpose of benefiting others—never from anger, violence, ignorance, or selfish motivations. Buddhas' wrathful expressions generate strength, joy, and wisdom—never violence, pain, or confusion.

Avalokiteshvara, besides being a Buddha in various forms, also appears in various other manifestations, including as a bodhisattva, a human being, an animal, and nature—or any merciful form that could potentially serve, guide, and protect those in need of his light of love. So some East Asian and Southeast Asian Buddhists pray to Kuan Yin as a bodhisattva. She is generally interpreted as being Avalokiteshvara in female form with two arms, either sitting or standing.[117]

Regardless of which form or name of the Buddha we use, if we could see him or her as the fully enlightened Buddha of Loving-Kindness and pray from the heart with fervent devotion and trust, then all forms will equally become the source of blessings and the support for attainments.

The Speech of the Buddha of Loving-Kindness

Hear all sounds as the pure natural sound of the Buddha's wisdom and love. The Buddha's speech resounds with sixty excellent qualities that fill the whole of existence. All sounds are his speech, the holy Dharma, and sounds of the sacred wisdom energy waves. Listen to the Buddha calling you—to awaken you and all trainable beings from their heavy stupor in the womb of ignorance. If we could realize sounds as such, as they are, then all the words, sounds, and expressions of the universe would arise for us as pure Buddha voices, the sound of Buddha wisdom in their true nature and quality.

The Mind of the Buddha of Loving-Kindness

The Buddha's mind is ever-open, ever-peaceful, and totally free from conceptual elaboration and afflicting emotions. He is beyond sensory dependence: he doesn't need the senses to communicate. He knows and reaches everything intimately and instantly through his omniscience. In the state of this ultimate boundless sphere, the union of the light of Buddha wisdom and the light of loving-kindness glows boundlessly forever, like the lights of the sun and moon. The union of omniscient wisdom and loving-kindness is the omnipresent wisdom-mind of the Buddha that pervades all phenomena and fulfills all the needs of every being spontaneously and effortlessly.

The Buddha of Loving-Kindness
Embodies All the Enlightened Ones

The Buddha of Loving-Kindness is not an individual Buddha or bodhisattva. He is the embodiment of all the Buddhas and bodhisattvas and the wisdom of all highly accomplished adepts. Besides that, he is the absolute and pure nature of all phenomenal existents, as they are. So feel that you are in the presence of the ultimate, boundless pure nature of all. Feel that whatever appears before you is the true nature and quality of the body, speech, and mind of the Buddha.

Amitabha, Avalokiteshvara, Tara, Shakyamuni Buddha, Guru Rinpoche, Yeshe Tshogyal, and the Enlightened Masters are simply different names and different forms of one essence—"Buddhaness." That is why Patrul Rinpoche wrote about the Buddha of Loving-Kindness as the unity of all the deities or Buddhas:

> The one deity in whom all deities are embodied is
> Avalokiteshvara.
> The one mantra in which all essences are included is
> the Six Syllables.
> The one Dharma in which all the development and
> perfection stages are completed is bodhichitta.
> So, in the [meditative] state of the Knowing One
> Who Liberates All, recite the Six Syllables.[118]

Mipham Rinpoche also writes:

> Whichever personal deity you pray to, in its true
> meaning it will be no different from praying to

the Buddha [Shakyamuni], for, as it is said, "All the Buddhas are the same in Dharmakaya." You must understand that the supreme Buddha has manifested in the form of this and that personal deity [*yidam*] to provide refuge and protection for us, the beings of this age of dregs. [However,] if you think that the Buddha and your personal deity are separate, and think that you are leaving the Buddha and picking another as your personal deity, then you will have a hard time attaining anything.[119]

So, we must pray to any Buddha as the embodiment of all the Enlightened Ones with total devotion and trust. The Third Dodrupchen prays:

When we are happy, you are the object of veneration and respect.
When we are suffering, you are the one to whom we lament.
While we are alive, you are the one we depend on.
And when we die, you are the one we take refuge in.
O Padmasambhava, Avalokiteshvara, and our Root Lama—
You are not separate, though you have separate names and forms.
I do not see you as separate individuals, but as one.
Please hold me tightly with your kindness—
I pray.[120]

Buddha Is Not Separate from You

Know that the Buddha is not a separate presence from you. Through the unmistaken path of devotional prayer, meditation, and trust, if you perfect your experience of loving-kindness, purify all your emotional and intellectual obscurations, and complete the dual accumulations of merits and wisdom, you will attain Buddhahood by just seeing the true nature of your own mind and its qualities, as well as the true face and qualities of the Buddha of Loving-Kindness, as they are.

If we realize the true nature of our own mind, we realize the true nature and qualities of all existents, which is Buddhahood. So the Buddha is not somewhere else. He is in us. He is our true nature.

If you keep focusing your mind one-pointedly on the presence of the Buddha of Loving-Kindness—or on some particular aspect of him, such as his loving-kindness or his eyes looking lovingly at us—then before long a powerful feeling of devotional energy is certain to emerge in your mindstream. Once that happens, a heat of joy and bliss will arise in every part of your mind and body because of a mental and physical suppleness such as you have never felt before. If you have already experienced this, it will augment the experience.

When this experience happens, you should allow the blissful heat generated by the development of loving-kindness to increase without grasping at or being attached to it. Then the precious bodhichitta unstained by the obscurations of defiled concepts will awaken in you. In the minds of those who follow the path of devotion, these enlightening effects will miraculously manifest before their own eyes.

Pray with Devotion

Visualize all this as clearly as you can, maintaining the image and feelings for as long as possible. Pray with devotion by focusing the heartfelt energy of your mind with all its six consciousnesses (eye, ear, nose, tongue, body, and mind) and the energies of every particle of our body with one-pointed trust in the Buddha of Loving-Kindness and his loving-kindness.

Then, singing the Six-Syllable Prayer[121]—OM MA-NI PAD-ME HUNG—loudly or silently in your mind's voice, pray to the Buddha, thinking, "O Buddha of Omniscient Wisdom and Loving-Kindness—please pay your kind attention to me and all mother-beings with your unconditional love. May your enlightened body, speech, and mind, and especially your unconditional love, take birth in our mindstreams this very moment." Then recite or chant the Six-Syllable Prayer with heartfelt devotion in the sweetest sound or melody, as many times as you can: OM MA-NI PAD-ME HUNG. (Please go online to http://www.shambhala.com/heartofunconditionallove for an audio sample.) Think and feel that every thought of your mind and every sound of the breathing of every particle of your body is peaceful, joyful, and bursting into the song of the prayer of loving-kindness. OM MA-NI PAD-ME HUNG.

Think and feel that every being of the universe—visible and invisible, large and small, even the smallest insect—is singing the prayer with heartfelt devotion to the

Buddha and enjoying the amazing warmth of his loving-kindness. OM MA-NI PAD-ME HUNG.

Hear and enjoy the sounds of the energy waves of every particle of nature as they are singing the prayer with the energy of joy and celebration, enjoying the sacred sounds and meanings of the prayer. OM MA-NI PAD-ME HUNG.

Hear every sound of the world as the singing sound of the prayer of loving-kindness. The whole universe is resounding with sounds of loving-kindness like a great symphony hall filled with harmonies of peace, joy, and love. There is nothing but the sound and feeling of loving-kindness. OM MA-NI PAD-ME HUNG.

When you focus on praying with the heart of total devotion and trust in the Buddha by enjoying his loving-kindness, then before long, unconditional love—the Buddha's blessings and loving-kindness—will take birth in you. You become what you are seeing, hearing, and feeling. As a popular proverb has it, "When you see the face of a laughing person, you too will start laughing. When you see the face of a crying person, you too will start crying."

As an indication of developing loving-kindness in your mindstream, you could suddenly experience an indescribable heat with joyfulness or blissfulness. Tears of joy might stream from your eyes. You could feel every hair of your body rising with a sense of celebrating the new birth of bodhichitta in you.

When you experience true trust and devotion in yourself as a result of your heartfelt prayers to the Buddha and his unconditional love, then loving-kindness will take birth in you, as you will have been transformed into the Buddha of Loving-Kindness himself.

Again, if you keep saying the prayers continuously with the same strong devotion and keep fully enjoying the blissful heat that is generated by the Buddha's love, then, like a child enjoying the taste of honey, before long the thought of loving-kindness will awaken in your mind spontaneously without any need of separate effort. You will then experience that your mind itself has arisen as the body of pure loving-kindness, as it is. You will feel that all your physical activities and vocal expressions have become the very expressions of loving-kindness.

The Meaning of the Six-Syllable Prayer

Recite or chant the Six-Syllable Prayer of the Buddha of Loving-Kindness, OM MA-NI PAD-ME HUNG, with heartfelt devotion in the sweetest sound or melody you can. OM MA-NI PAD-ME HUNG is the heart essence of all the teachings, both exoteric (Sutra) and esoteric (Tantra), of Mahayana Buddhism.

Although it has only a few syllables, this prayer is the distillation of the wisdom and loving-kindness of all the Buddhas. It is the essence of the Buddha of Loving-Kindness manifested in the form of sacred words, sound, and letters. It is the profound sound of the ultimate nature.

Sing or chant the sacred prayer with the energy of devotion and trust in the Buddha. Your mind fully blossoms with the Buddha's blessing energies and the power of your own devotion. As a result, whatever you say or hear becomes the expression and sound of sacred innate prayer and leads you to enlightenment. It is said that whoever sees the images of the Six Syllables or pronounces them with devotion will attain liberation by seeing and saying them. Whoever appreciates the meaning of the Six Syllables will attain liberation by understanding them. The prayer's meaning is vast and profound and it is abundant with power, yet it is easy to say and remember. It can easily be chanted by young and old, educated or illiterate, ordained or lay, and will lead us from happiness to enlightenment.

OM is a composite of three letters or sounds: AH + O + M. These three Sanskrit letters symbolize, represent, or embody the body, speech, and wisdom mind of the Buddha of Loving-Kindness, as well as our own body, speech, and mind. Also, the joining of AH, O, and M together symbolizes the indivisible nature of the Buddha's body, speech, and mind.

OM is sometimes also used as the expression for invoking the Buddha with devotion and initiating auspicious celebrations.

MANI means gem or jewel, symbolizing wisdom.[122] Here, the gem (*mani*) that the Buddha holds between the palms of his first two hands symbolizes or represents the Buddha's wisdom that is free from concepts, yet fulfills all the wishes and needs of beings with its great power.

PADME means flower or lotus, which symbolizes loving-kindness.[123] The flower (*padme*) that the Buddha holds in his second left hand symbolizes his loving-kindness that brings joy to all, yet remains unstained by conceptual or emotional impurities, for the essence of loving-kindness is the essence of wisdom.[124] When loving-kindness appears among beings to serve them, it remains pure, for its suchness is free from the dual obscurations.[125] Loving-kindness is thus symbolized by the lotus flower because even though the roots of the lotus grow in mud, the flower remains pure and unstained. The union of wisdom (*mani*) and loving-kindness (*padme*) is the path and the goal of enlightenment to be attained. The flower also symbolizes loving-kindness, compassion, and skillful means.

Phonologically, *padma* is the lotus, and the *e* vowel at the end of *padme* changes it to the vocative, the grammatical case for addressing and invoking (in this case, addressing the Buddha).

HUNG (or HUM) is pronounced *hoong*. It symbolizes the twofold innate wisdom or mind of the Buddha—the wisdom that knows all things as they are, in detail, and the wisdom that knows the true nature of all, as it is. It also symbolizes the five wisdoms or the five aspects of the Buddha or Buddha wisdom:

1. Ultimate wisdom: the openness or emptiness aspect of wisdom
2. Mirror-like wisdom: the aspect of wisdom that enables all to arise and function spontaneously
3. Wisdom of equality: the aspect of remaining in the all-evenness state
4. Discriminative wisdom: the aspect of knowing all (omniscience)

5. All-accomplishing wisdom: the aspect that accomplishes all Buddha actions, services, and purposes

HUNG is the ultimate, natural, and sacred sound that invokes the mind of the Buddha. It also embodies the bodhichitta of the Buddha. HUNG symbolizes the meaning of suchness, the nondual state, the ultimate goal to be realized through meditation.

When reciting the Six-Syllable Prayer, feel and think about as many of its meanings as you can. You could recite the Six Syllables in any of the following ways:

- As a way of calling to the Buddha for his blessings, guidance, and protection
- As an exercise in opening and vitalizing your enlightening energy waves
- As a way to empower yourself to remain in absorption
- As a way to empower and transform all into Buddha blessing

There are numerous other interpretations of the Six-Syllable Prayer:

OM, "Oh, embodiment of the body, speech, and mind aspects of all the Buddhas"; MA-NI PAD-ME, "who holds a gem and lotus" [or "who is the union of wisdom and skillful means"]; HUNG, "please look at me and all mother-beings with your loving-kindness."

OM, Our body, speech, and mind, and the body, speech, and mind of the Buddha; through MA-NI, the wisdom [or emptiness] and PAD-ME, loving-kind-ness; HUNG, may they be united.

OM, The embodiment of all the Buddhas; MA-NI PAD-ME, who holds a gem [wisdom] and flower [lov-ing-kindness]; HUNG, [to you] I pray.

OM, The embodiment of all the Buddhas; MA-NI PAD-ME, the lord of all-knowing wisdom and lov-ing-kindness; HUNG, [to you] I pray.

OM, Buddha(s); MA-NI PAD-ME, the lord of all-know-ing wisdom and loving-kindness; HUNG, please be-hold us with your omniscient wisdom.

OM, Buddha; MA-NI PAD-ME, who holds a lotus and gem; HUNG, in the expanse of your mind I contemplate.

OM, Buddha; MA-NI PAD-ME, the wisdom and skill-ful means; HUNG, in the expanse of their unity I con-template.

OM, Oh, MA-NI PAD-ME, the holder of the gem and lotus; HUNG, [to you] I pray.

OM, Oh, MA-NI PAD-ME, the lord of wisdom and lov-ing-kindness; HUNG, [to you] I pray.

OM, Oh, MA-NI PAD-ME, the lord of wisdom and lov-ing-kindness; HUNG, please, behold us.

OM, Oh, MA-NI PAD-ME, the lord of wisdom and lov-ing-kindness; HUNG, please grant the realization of nondual wisdom.

A number of sources say that PAD-ME symbolizes or represents wisdom and MA-NI symbolizes skillful means, such as compassion and loving-kindness. I have adopted that interpretation in previous books. However, in this book, I follow the detailed interpretations of MA-NI and PAD-ME given by the Third Dodrupchen Rinpoche.[126] He writes:

> MA-NI is the perfection of wisdom, as it has no concepts and has inconceivable power. PAD-ME is the great compassion, as it arises by relying upon or thinking of swamp-like samsara and it pleases all beings.[127]

Nevertheless, the essence of both my former and current interpretations is to teach the meaning of the union of omniscient wisdom (emptiness) and loving-kindness (skillful means) of Buddhahood through the symbols of gems and flowers.

There are also many teachings on seeing the Six Syllables as the Six Perfections—generosity, discipline, patience, diligence, contemplation, and wisdom. There are meditations on lights coming from each syllable and accomplishing the goals of purification and attainment.

Ter texts often add a HRI syllable at the end of the Six-Syllable Prayer, making it a seven-syllable prayer: OM MA-NI PAD-ME HUNG HRI. The HRI symbolizes the heart-seed syllable of the Buddha of Loving-Kindness. The first Six Syllables are the part of prayer that invokes; the HRI syllable symbolizes the mind of the Buddha, which is to be invoked.

If we could spend our life chanting or singing the six- or seven-syllable prayer with total devotion to the Buddha and total loving-kindness to all mother-beings, we would attain the fruits of many teachings. To chant like this would be to experience the enlightened heart-essences of all the Dharma teachings, such as devotion, loving-kindness, and wisdom. It would transform our body, speech, and mind into Buddha and Dharma.

People who recite the Six-Syllable Prayer with devotion and loving-kindness as their everyday prayer will gradually and naturally attain endless spiritual accomplishments. They will eventually become free from sick mentalities like grasping at "self," arrogance, hatred, craving, and obsessive sensations.

Receiving Purifications and Blessings

Visualize and repeatedly generate devotion toward and trust in the Buddha of Loving-Kindness. Then visualize that from his body, the blessings of his body, speech, and mind—and of his wisdom, love, and power in general, and particularly the power of his loving-kindness—are projected in various forms of rainbow-beam-like lights with blissful heat. The waves of beams and rays come toward you with the sweet, soothing sound of the Six-Syllable Prayer. They enter you through every pore of your body. Your body is completely filled with the flood of the radiant blessing light with blissful heat and the soothing sounds of the Six Syllables, like a vase filled with nectar.

Again and again, think and feel that the beams of blessing light of the Buddha's wisdom, love, and power and especially his loving-kindness have filled your body with inconceivable radiance and blissful heat and the feeling of unconditional love. Feel and believe that these blessing lights have completely purified all your ignorant mental qualities rooted in grasping at "self," all the negative karma that you've ever accumulated, all your emotional and intellectual obscurations with their habitual tendencies, and all their undesirable effects—sickness, sadness, and fear that have until now filled our minds and bodies in the form of total darkness. Then think and feel again and again that this darkness within you is completely dispelled, without a trace, thanks to the power of the bright wisdom blessing light. Repeatedly recognize and enjoy the absence of that darkness, or ill-effects, and celebrate in the brightness of the blessing light of absolute love.

See, feel, and trust that not only are your negative mentalities and bodily ills purified and exhausted, but also that each particle of your body has become immaculate, transparent, and boundless like the clear sky. Every particle of your body is now transformed into a particle of radiant blessing light of loving-kindness of the Buddha.

The movements of your inhalations and exhalations, the waves of every particle of your body, become the energy waves of blissful heat of wisdom and loving-kindness—the blessings of the Buddha. Every blessing wave emits infinite dazzling rays with blissful heat and gentle or roaring sounds of the Six-Syllable Prayer. Think and believe that the unconditional love of the Buddha of Loving-Kindness has merged with your own mind and remains inseparable, as one. All your thoughts have become the thoughts of loving-kindness, wishing immeasurable joy and happiness forever for all infinite beings of the universe.

The waves of your body and physical activities also become the waves of the power of loving-kindness that fulfills the wishes and needs of all beings. You have the power to fulfill others' wishes because of the power of loving-kindness that came from the Buddha and that has awakened and blossomed in you.

7

MEDITATION ON THE
INNER BUDDHA

THE INNER BUDDHA Stage is about recognizing Buddha qualities in your own mind.

Awaken the Realization of Loving-Kindness in Yourself

Before starting, remember and calmly focus your attention on what you have experienced in your body in the first stage.

Then recognize and feel that your ordinary thoughts and feelings have awakened into thoughts and feelings of openness wisdom, boundless power, and especially unconditional love—triggered by seeing and feeling them in the external Buddha. Think, feel, and recognize these boundless Buddha qualities in your every thought, every bodily particle, and every wave of your breathing with the sound of the Six Syllables—over and over again.

See that your mind and body have turned into light—light of the Buddha's wisdom, power, and loving-kindness. Inconceivable beams of blessing lights of loving-kindness, filled with blissful heat with sweet sounds of the sacred Six-Syllable Prayer, emanate from your body. These light beams are, in fact, the blessing energies of the Buddha's unconditional love.

Extend Loving-Kindness to Others

Having awakened and anchored the realization of loving-kindness within ourselves, we must now share those blessings with others, step by step. We begin with a loved one, then distant acquaintances, then strangers, then those we don't like, and finally all infinite beings—bringing the Buddha's lights and/or lights from our own blessed hearts to purify and enlighten each group in turn.

The Mother as Our Focal Point

So we start by focusing on a loved one, such as our mother. Tibetans generally use the mother to inspire them to awaken loving-kindness. She is regarded as the greatest symbol of love and care to us, her children, and a symbol of love in general. The mother is seen as an all-important and powerful teacher for us to understand and generate pure love loving-kindness.

Unfortunately, a lot of people do not have a relationship based on love and respect with their mothers. If so, they should substitute her with someone else whom they love and respect. Eventually, though, we should try to appreciate everyone, including our mother, as a source of inspiration and object of loving-kindness meditation, as she is the one who gave us our precious life and cherished us.

Many people want to use their husband, wife, boyfriend, or girlfriend as their initial source of inspiration to practice, because they love them more than anyone else. If your love for these people is pure, then by all means choose them. Unfortunately, however, what you feel toward your romantic partner could be more attachment or lust rooted in the tight grip of grasping at ego, rather than pure love. If so, and if you meditate on them, they could become a source of beastly attachment, craving, and obsession that will end up causing you and them pain sooner or later. So, when you start learning how to meditate on loving-kindness, it is best not to use your intimate partner as your inspiration. Instead, pick someone who opens pure loving-kindness in you without tightening your attachment.

How to Generate Loving-Kindness toward Your Mother

So start with your mother (or a substitute) and reflect on the true loving qualities of all that she gave you. Remember and feel her kindness from the bottom of your heart—her kindness in giving you your body, giving you life, caring for you through so many hardships, teaching you how to handle life step-by-step, and training you to defend yourself from adversities, small and big.

Think about and feel from the heart the many sacrifices she endured for you over the years. Think about how she deprived herself of true happiness and the sources of true happiness for your sake. If you think about these things seriously, you will notice arising within you an unbearable urge to repay her kindness by dedicating every waking hour of your life, every ounce of your energy, to improving her life. When you experience this heartfelt love toward her, repeatedly express this heartfelt wish: "May my mother have true happiness and the cause of happiness." Make a heartfelt commitment: "I will dedicate my whole life to bringing true happiness to her life."

Then pray to the Buddha of Loving-Kindness from the depth of your being for his help, his blessings: "O Buddha of Loving-Kindness! Please look after my mother with unconditional love. Please bestow on her all your kind blessings so that she may enjoy happiness now and attain enlightenment before long."

To maintain and strengthen your own feelings, now and then rekindle your devotion in the Buddha and his love, by thinking about and feeling his extraordinary loving-kindness and compassion to you.

How to Bring Blessing Lights to Your Mother

Now visualize that infinite beams and rays of blessing lights of unconditional love in various colors come from the Buddha of Loving-Kindness, whom you have visualized before you, and enter your mother. If you like, you can also see lights projecting from your own heart and body to your mother—as you have awakened yourself as a body and mind of Buddha blessings.

See the radiant and blazing blessing lights fill her body, purifying, healing, and transforming her every particle—as you did for yourself in the Outer Buddha Stage. All the sickness, sadness, and impurities of her mind and body, which assume the form of darkness in her body, are fully dispelled and purified by the power of blessing light. All her unwholesome concepts, emotions, and sensations become the Buddha's radiant loving-kindness. All her virtuous wishes are fulfilled. All the particles of her body awaken into particles of the blessing light of the Buddha's all-knowing wisdom, loving-kindness, and boundless power.

How to Meditate on Lights

Buddhist meditation Masters describe how to meditate on the lights projecting from Buddhas. The Buddhas' names may differ, but the principle remains the same. Karma Chagme Rinpoche[128] describes how to meditate on the lights projecting from the Healing Buddha:

> Lights of lapis-like color are projected.
> They merge into oneself and the devotees.
> Everyone's sicknesses are dissolved like frost touched
>   by sunlight.[129]

Mipham Rinpoche describes how to meditate on lights projecting from Shakyamuni Buddha:

> While you are pronouncing the Buddha's name and reciting his *dharani*,[130] [imagine that] from his body he projects his great wisdom-lights in various colors. They dispel all your and beings' obscurations. All beings have perfectly realized all the attainments of the Mahayana path and achieved the stage of nonreturners.[131]

The Third Dodrupchen teaches how to meditate on lights projecting from Amitabha, the Buddha of Infinite Light:

Reciting [the prayer] with a one-pointed mind,
Invoke the mind of the Buddha and his disciples.
[Think that] from their bodies rays of light are
    emitted.
They pacify all one's own and others' suffering, and
Accomplish all the aspirations that we all have
    made.[132]

EXTEND LOVING-KINDNESS TO FRIENDS, STRANGERS, FOES, AND ALL BEINGS

Now reflect that there is not a single being who hasn't been your kind mother during one or other of your infinite previous lives, as discussed in chapter 4. Like your present mother, these beings were kind to you, took care of you and made tremendous sacrifices for you. They all need happiness, just like your present mother.

Use the same formula—generating the same loving-kindness as you felt for your mother and sharing blessing lights from the Buddha and/or from yourself—to each of the following groups in sequence: friends, then neutral beings (strangers), then your so-called foes, and finally all infinite beings.

Take time to deepen the feeling of your unconditional love for each group. Try to develop a heartfelt loving-kindness toward each group before moving on to the next, as much as you can. Take time to purify and transform each group until you feel that all beings are transformed into the minds of loving-kindness and the bodies of blessing light of the Buddha and his Pure Land.

It might take a lot of effort to generate loving-kindness

to your foes. But according to Buddhism, they too must have been your loving mothers once upon a time. The more angry and mean they are to you now, the more loving-kindness you owe them, for, like butterflies flying to candle flames, they are rushing toward a harsher and bleaker future due to their ignorance-driven misdeeds.

Conclude the meditation by visualizing, feeling, and believing that all beings and the whole universe have been purified, healed, and transformed into a universe of blessing light with boundless peace, joy, and unconditional love—the qualities of the Buddha of Loving-Kindness.

In this Inner Buddha meditation, you are generating heartfelt loving-kindness—aspirations for beings to have happiness and attain enlightenment. You are also putting those aspirations into practice by praying and doing the meditation, which embodies the qualities of the Six Perfections of the bodhisattva path.

8

MEDITATION ON THE
UNIVERSAL BUDDHA

IN THE UNIVERSAL BUDDHA STAGE we perceive all form—our body, the universe—as the image of the Buddha and his Pure Land with the qualities of loving-kindness. We hear all sound—within us and without—as the sound of the Six-Syllable Mantra, waves of the sound of loving-kindness. We experience all feelings—meditation, emotions, and sensations—as the feeling and expression of unconditional love.

Seeing, Hearing, and Feeling Every Particle of Your
Body as a Boundless Pure Land of Loving-Kindness

Remember that your mind has been transformed into a mind of Buddha blessings, loving-kindness. Remember to see and feel that your body—your whole body—has become the body of Buddha's blessing light, light of loving-kindness, as described in the last chapter.

So, now, see and experience every particle of your body as a particle of blessing light. Every particle of light is an inconceivably vast pure land. Each pure land is presided over by a Buddha of Loving-Kindness. Each pure land is filled with infinite Buddhas, bodhisattvas, *dakas,* and *dakinis,* who have all-knowing wisdom, unconditional love, and boundless power.

Feel that all the movements of light, energy, and sound of your body's pure lands are waves of wisdom, love, and power with blissful heat—the blessing energies of the Buddhas and their pure lands. Every pure land is filled with singing and dancing angels—arisen as a great miraculous display. Even the music and dances of the celestial realms cannot compare. Every movement is accompanied by waves of blessing energies with the sweet music of holy Dharma—of esoteric teachings and prayers—that fill all the ten quarters.

See the magnificence, beauty, richness, and joyful nature of your body. Feel the vast magnitude of its infinite pure lands. When you are enjoying the amazing qualities of your body of light and love, your mind also spontaneously awakens into one of boundless loving-kindness, as mind is the one imagining and enjoying the infinite loving-kindness of the Buddha and pure lands.

At the beginning, you might find it challenging to wrap your head around the infinitude of boundless Buddha pure lands in the meditation. But you're not doing this exercise just for mental gymnastics to push the strength of your imagination. You're doing this exercise because boundless infinitude is, in fact, the absolute dimension of the pure lands. If, with a relaxed mind, you train yourself to conceive of such infinitude, the scope of your mind will open enormously because of the skill and power of such an approach.

Teaching on how to meditate on infinite pure lands, the Buddha himself said:

Imagine that on each atom there are as many
    Buddhas as the number of atoms in the world
Sitting in the midst of [an ocean of] their children
    [disciples].
Thus the entire atmosphere
Is filled with infinite Buddhas.
An ocean of inexhaustible tributes
Of all those Buddhas is expressed
Through the sounds of an ocean of melodies.
I praise all the Bliss Gones.[133] . . .
On each atom there are as many pure lands as the
    number of atoms in the world.
In each pure land, there are infinite Buddhas
Sitting in the midst of their children [disciples].
May I see them and perform enlightened activities
    with them.[134]

The Buddha also said:

Learn to enter into the thought of [seeing]
    inconceivable pure lands of the Buddhas within
    the dimensions of a single hair.
. . . .
[See] that your own body is fully filled with Buddha
    pure lands.[135]

Again, the Buddha said:

In the space of a single hair, [see] as many Buddhas
As the number of sand particles of the Ganges River.
Each Buddha has that many pure lands.

Meditation on the Universal Buddha · 123

Each has its own unique characteristics and
qualities.[136]

Seeing, Hearing, and Feeling Every Particle of the World as Boundless Pure Lands of Loving-Kindness

Once you have trained your mind to see your body as a
body of loving-kindness made of infinite Buddha pure
lands, start seeing the external world that way, too.

Whatever you see—beings, land, mountains, flowers,
houses—see as appearances of loving-kindness, the Buddha of Loving-Kindness and his Pure Land. Whatever
you hear—people, nature, traffic, music, prayers—hear
as sound with the quality of loving-kindness, such as the
sound of the Six-Syllable Mantra. Whatever you feel—
whether mentally, physically, or emotionally—experience
it with the qualities of loving-kindness, for the Buddha of
Loving-Kindness is reaching and uniting with all, as discussed in the Inner Buddha Stage. Before long, all beings
and the world will arise for you with the qualities of loving-kindness—or even as loving-kindness free from concepts (the final Universal Buddha Stage, discussed in the
next chapter).

Again, see each wave of your mind of loving-kindness
as a projecting and gathering of rays of light of unconditional love. Perceive each wave of your exhalation and
inhalation as sending and receiving waves of light with
blissful heat of the wisdom body of the Buddha of Loving-Kindness. Experience each wave of natural sound of
the Buddha's speech, the sacred Six Syllables, as filling all

existents with boundless power. Feel the omnipresent wisdom of enlightened nature and qualities of the Buddha pervading all as the union of loving-kindness and emptiness.

Realizing and remaining in the awakened nature of the Buddha body, speech, and mind, chant or sing the sacred Six-Syllable Prayer slowly and softly, clearly, and accurately in the sweetest melody you can, hundreds, thousands, millions of times: OM MA-NI PAD-ME HUNG.

When you are enlightened, loving-kindness and blessing lights are the same in their ultimate nature. They are Buddha and Buddha pure lands. They are Buddha wisdom, love, and action. They are the nature of the universe: infinitely open, pure, radiant, omnipresent, and nondual.

Until we are highly realized, we should visualize blessing lights as rainbow lights or as the light of the sun or moon, which are relatively subtle and pure. As we advance, we should try to realize blessing lights as the Buddha's wisdom, love, and power—as accomplishing everything, fulfilling our wishes, and enlightening all. The Buddha said:

The body of the Buddha emits lights
As numerous as the atoms of [the earth multiplied by a]
    hundred thousand of the number of particles [of
    the ocean].
Likewise, the number of pure lands are as infinite
    as . . .
The number of particles in the ocean.
There are as many [rays of] light [as there are] atoms.
Each [light ray has] many secondary rays.
These lights manifest pure forms of Buddhas

In lands where there are no Buddhas
[So that they can] teach the most profound
    Dharma.[137]

These lights are pure, boundless, and beyond conceptual mind. They are the source of peace, joy, and realization. The Buddha taught:

In brief, these lights [of the Buddha] transcend all
    lights.
These lights are immaculate. They are totally vast.
They cause bliss in the body and joy to the mind. . . .
They generate joy, supreme joy, and bliss.
For beings whose minds are virtuous, they cause
    them to have virtues, vast realization,
Knowledge, and supreme joy in their minds.[138]

Je Tsongkhapa writes:

These lights are immaculate like crystal. They are
thoroughly vast like space. They cause bliss in the
body. They cause joy in the mind. Whomever they
touch, they make supremely joyful.[139]

Filling the days of our lives with devotional meditations, loving-kindness, and heartfelt prayers is the way to triumphantly fulfill the goal of our precious life.

9

MEDITATION ON THE
ULTIMATE BUDDHA

The Ultimate Buddha Stage is about meditating on loving-kindness free from concepts. This is the union of loving-kindness qualities and the openness nature that we realize if our meditation on loving-kindness has progressed well and reached the final stage of attainment.

*Rest in the Awareness of Boundless Loving-Kindness
without Grasping*

So now, meditate as follows. When you were meditating on the Universal Buddha Stage, you might have experienced an awareness of loving-kindness that was openness and boundlessness. To bring that to the Ultimate Buddha Stage, when that happens, don't grasp at the experience at that moment. Just remain open. Don't conceptualize or label it. Just rest in stillness. Don't let your mind waver with thoughts. Just remain tranquil. Don't entertain doubts or expectations. Just relax. Rest in the state of mere awakened awareness of boundless loving-kindness without thoughts.

With openness, watch the openness nature—the see-ingness and knowingness of the innate loving-kindness—without apprehension, modification, hesitation, expectation, or fixation. Rest in such openness state, as it is. Let the chain of conceptual thoughts break, melt, and dissolve naturally and simultaneously like a mirage.

When you experience the awakened openness state of mind, remain in it without dualistic thoughts. Don't let your mind run after past thoughts or memories. Don't invite future thoughts or dreams. Don't grasp at any present thought. Just remain in the awakened state of loving-kindness free from concepts, as it is, where there is no root that produces any thought, and no foundation that provides any ground for thought to dwell. When the realization of this awakened state is fully perfected, it will blossom as the omniscient wisdom with fivefold dimensionless dimension.[140]

Expand the Ultimate Resting in the Awareness of All

After gaining some stability in this meditative state, you could introduce more meditation exercises to expand the depth, breadth, power, and actions of the experience.

In their true nature, all remain in the union of loving-kindness and emptiness. So see all the images that appear before you as the union of appearances and emptiness that are boundlessly open. Hear all the sounds that you hear as the soothing sound of Dharma, the union of sound and emptiness. Understand all your thoughts as the great union of awareness and emptiness, or loving-kindness free from concepts. Experience all your experiences as the powerful waves of blissful heat, the union of bliss and emptiness. Meditate on this over and over again.

Recognize and remain in the awareness of such union—the ultimate loving-kindness. Repeatedly chant or sing the sacred Six-Syllable Prayer slowly and softly in the sweetest melody with total openness—the great boundless unity of sound and emptiness: OM MA-NI PAD-ME HUNG.

Instructions and Benefits as Taught in the Sacred Teachings

Longchen Rabjam advises that after meditating on loving-kindness that is with concepts, we must contemplate loving-kindness that is free from concepts and rest in it. He writes:

> After that, contemplate in the all-evenness state. That is great loving-kindness free from concepts, as it is the union of loving-kindness and emptiness. The objects of loving-kindness, beings, have taken birth due to the gathering of earth, water, fire, air, space, and consciousness. But if you analyze them, they exist neither as gross elements, subtle absolute reality, nor consciousness. They are like space. Thinking thus, meditate on this. . . . When beings appear, if you analyze their bodies, you will not find their existence. You will find neither a consciousness that depends on [a body] nor a body [on which a mind] is depended. In this way you will not find any "I" or "my," as they are emptiness in their true nature. . . . Merely appearing to be seen or heard does not prove something true or false. True or false is a thing invented by the mind. . . . As the sign of the perfection of the meditation—while the development of loving-kindness [toward all is present] in you—you

have the concurrent realization that there is no reality or self in beings, like a water-tree.[141]

If you maintain such a meditative state, then due to the power of (1) the blessings of the Buddha of Loving-Kindness and (2) the virtue of doing meditations on loving-kindness and loving-kindness that is free from concepts, we will realize the ultimate meaning, loving-kindness whose essence is emptiness. That is the suchness—the true nature of all that is free from conceptual elaboration. It is the loving-kindness that is free from concepts. It is also the true nature of the mind, the state that is free since the beginning. When you realize such true nature, you must maintain that realization by remaining in it through meditation without wavering until the full realization is perfected.

Then gradually, as the self-power of that realization, all phenomenal appearances will start arising as the Buddha of Loving-Kindness and his radiant Pure Land, spontaneously. Then all appear, but with no duality, as they are pure and open. All function, but without distinctions of good and bad. All arise, but naturally free and fully complete, without any limitation or conflict. This experience is the total freedom from the dual obscurations—emotional and intellectual—without even a trace of duality. Such realization will awaken the two wisdoms—the wisdom of knowing all things as they are, and the wisdom of knowing the truth of all as it is. That is also the securing of the fully enlightened state, the primordial nature.

In the state of such realization, all thoughts of grasping at physical and nonphysical objects have been exhausted, verbal designations and conceptual thoughts have ceased, and all suffering and conflict have ended. This is known as the Great Wisdom Mother (Prajnaparamita). Nagarjuna writes:

> The expiration of grasping at physical and
>   nonphysical objects
> Is called the cessation of suffering.[142]

Shantideva writes:

> When something and no-thing
> Are not there before your mind [to apprehend],
> Then there will be no other option [for your mind,
>   except to]
> Rest in peace, free from concepts.[143]

Ngulchu Thogme[144] writes:

> All that appears is [the creation of] one's mind.
> The nature of the mind is free from extremes from the
>   beginning.
> Having realized this, never think about the
>   characteristics of grasper or grasped.
> This is the practice of bodhisattvas.[145]

This is the wisdom that is nondual, free from the two extremes. It is free from falling into eternalism, as it is emptiness like space. It is free from falling into nihilism, as it is the self-awareness or the discriminative (all-knowing) wisdom. In the *Drachen Dzinkyi Yumla Todpa* sutra it is said:

Perfect wisdom is the freedom from designations and
concepts.
It is unborn and unceasing like the nature of space.
It can be seen through natural awareness, omniscient
wisdom.
It is the "Great Wisdom Mother" of the three times.
To you I pray.[146]

Maitreya-natha writes:

In this, there is nothing to be rejected
And nothing to be defended, even in the slightest.
Just look at the true suchness perfectly.
If you see it correctly, you are fully liberated.[147]

Training in the meaning of the union of loving-kindness and emptiness will lead us to realize the space-like
all-evenness state of all phenomenal existents. Giving
teachings on Dzogpa Chenpo meditation to Manjushrimitra,[148] Prahevajra[149] said:

The nature of the mind is Buddha from primordial
time.
Mind has no birth or cessation, like space.
Having realized the evenness state of all existents,
Remain in it, without seeking anything. That is the
meditation.[150]

So, if you realize the meaning of loving-kindness
free from concepts, you will have realized the meaning of
suchness, no-self,[151] freedom from extremes, universality,

and freedom from the beginning. You will have attained the sublime fruits that are taught in Madhyamaka, Mahamudra, and Dzogpa Chenpo. As Rigdzin Jigme Lingpa writes:

> Not dwelling in extremes is the meaning of Madhyamaka.
> Universality and spontaneity is the state of Mahamudra.
> Free from extremes and vastly open is the essential point of Dzogpa Chenpo.
> In this spontaneously perfect womb, where all the virtues of the paths and stages are complete from the origin,
> May I secure the Kingdom, the result.[152]

In brief, the loving-kindness that is free from concepts is the union of loving-kindness and emptiness wisdom. It is free from the concepts of subjective and objective elaboration. There is no inflaming of sensations, as it is free from the duality of players and things to be played. At the same time, it is not a neutral state—some kind of spacing out, unconscious, sleepy, or limbo state—as it is the natural awareness state of the boundlessly awakened wisdom with the essence of loving-kindness. It is fully open and all-knowing, as it is free from the constraints and confinements that are imposed by dualistic concepts and afflicting emotions.

Nevertheless, it is almost impossible for us beginners to even comprehend the idea of seeing anything through nonduality, as we are completely indoctrinated in dualistic, conceptual, and emotional and mental apparatuses. But if you realize the true wisdom that sees all through nondual wisdom eyes, that is free from the triple cycle of grasper, grasped, and grasping, then knowing all as one unity will be the natural way for you to see. It is the simplest yet most profound state to be in. Then the natural radiance of the nondual wisdom will remain blossoming boundlessly as your own ever-present wisdom-light.

The practices of Buddhism's "three disciplines" are encompassed within loving-kindness and its actions:

1. Meditating on the "four virtuous attitudes" (see chapter 4), and abandoning all thoughts and actions of harming others, is the discipline of the path of individual liberation (Skt. *pratimoksha*). This is the path of the Theravada tradition.
2. Training in bodhichitta and serving the needs of all is the bodhisattva discipline—the path of the Mahayana tradition.
3. Meditating on your own "three doors" as the sacred body, speech, and mind of the Buddha and attaining the union of wisdom and loving-kindness free from concepts is the esoteric discipline—the path of the Vajrayana tradition.

Nonetheless, until you are ready to realize nondual wisdom, unity with Buddha, you must totally rely on meditations that employ dualistic and conceptual devotion and loving-kindness, as they will lead you toward that true union gradually, safely, securely, and surely.

In the past, teachers often had to persuade their students to move to higher levels of meditations, as students were usually humble and cautious. Today, however, even beginners want to practice only the highest meditations, like the loving-kindness free from concepts or emptiness. They dive into ocean-like meditations without any clue of their depths, whether due to arrogance or being unrealistic.

The problem is that, if you try to meditate on high teachings like emptiness without adequate preparation from the ground level, you could very easily fall into the extreme views and experiences of nihilism or eternalism, while holding on to a subtle concept or thought of grasping at "a nothing" or "a non-existence." Or you could become lost in a state of being spaced out, with your mind endlessly floating semi-unconsciously, while you are not aware of anything. If these errors occur, though you might not be committing any gross misdeeds, you would still be very much recycling yourself in the chain of ignorance and confusion, which drag you further from the light of wisdom. True realization is the realization of the union of freedom from grasping at anything and the wisdom of self-awareness. But, again, high realizations will not take place unless you have vigorously trained in the preliminary trainings for a long time. Being smart, prosperous, youthful, or powerful cannot buy true realization.

10

Enhance the Effects

There are a number of things we can do during and after meditating to enhance its effects and guard against pitfalls.

Rejoicing

First, rejoicing magnifies the beneficial effects of these meditations. When we are self-critical—thinking, say, that our meditation was too short or not good enough—we take away from its power to help us. Instead, we should rejoice over the blessing energies of joy that free us from our mental tightness, confinement, conflicts, and clashes, and open us to the experience of a new dawn of peace, joy, and confidence. We can actually meditate on rejoicing over any wholesome action, thought, or experience to strengthen its benefits.

Recognizing Progress

Second, we should always recognize whatever meditation progress we experience. Doing this will strengthen the experience, hasten our progress, and refine its quality.

Remembering the Experience to Keep It Alive

Third, we should use memory and mindfulness to keep our meditation experiences alive. We don't just fill our body and mind with the blessing light of loving-kindness and the power of blissful heat and then rapidly move on to something else. Instead, we keep the experience alive by contemplating it again and again. Memory has three aspects: not forgetting, being familiar, and not wavering from the memory. Asanga[153] writes:

> What is memory? It is not forgetting a familiar object. It functions without wavering.[154]

By recalling our meditative experience and remaining in it without wavering, the experience anchors more deeply in our minds and displaces any lingering residues of impurities.

Protecting the Mind from Negative Experiences

Fourth, we must be careful to protect our minds from negative mentalities and emotions such as anger and attachment, and preserve our virtuous thoughts and emotions such as loving-kindness and devotion. We do this through mindfulness. Shantideva writes:

> If your wild elephant-like mind is tied
> With the ropes of mindfulness,
> Then all the dangers will disappear and
> All the virtues come into your hands. . . .

Untamed beings are unlimited as space,
You will never be able to overcome all.
Yet, if you could only overcome your hating mind,
Then you will find it as if you have overcome them all.

[For example,] where is the leather
With which you can cover the earth?
But if you just wear a leather sandal,
You will find it as if the earth has been covered.

Likewise, you will not be able to change
All the external objects,
But if you just change your own mind,
There is no need to change anything else.[155]

Exercising Caution about Devotion to Ordinary Objects

Finally, let me sound a word of caution about devotion to ordinary objects. While it is true that if we have devotion toward any object, even an ordinary one, we will benefit from it because of our mind's pure perception, an ordinary object still won't benefit us as much as an object that is truly enlightened. An enlightened object carries great blessings. So although it is good to have positive perception toward everything, we should spend more time and energy on sources of true blessings.

Also, if the object of our devotion is really negative, it could affect us negatively, directly and indirectly, if we are beginners. So, while we should respect and love all, we should make sure to stay with true spiritual sources, at least until we are very highly accomplished.

11

MOVE FORWARD STEP BY STEP

Advance Step by Step, in Sequence

It is important to stick with the step-by-step progression of the meditations in this book. Build a solid foundation of trust and devotion to the Outer Buddha in the first stage before focusing too much on the subsequent stages. And when you develop loving-kindness, start with one loved one before including a boundless audience. If you start with a boundless number of beings, your feelings of loving-kindness might be superficial, vague, and generalized—rather than deep, authentic, and personal. Then, even if you want to go back to meditating on one individual at a time, you might feel numb or as if you were new to the meditation. So, as Je Tsongkhapa writes:

> Without individualizing, if you train to meditate [on loving-kindness] toward all beings in general from the beginning, then even if you feel that loving-kindness has arisen in you, when you meditate on an individual being, you will find that loving-kindness has, in fact, never been developed in you. So you must develop a mind that will give you

a transformative experience by doing [loving-kind-ness] meditation on an individual person. . . . Then slowly increase the number of people on whom you focus in your meditation. At the end, focus on all in general. Thereafter, loving-kindness will arise in you whether you are focusing on an individual person or on all in general.[156]

Elevate Your Training as Your Experiences Improve

How quickly should you go through each stage? That depends solely on how deep and strong your existing meditation experiences and attainments are. Until you are ready, you must exert yourself in the stage on which you are working.

Buddhist trainees like me have supposedly been pursuing the right trainings consistently from day one, since we met the Dharma. In reality, however, we exhaust the cycle of days and nights of our lives by carelessly indulging in endless mundane activities, such as the ten mental, vocal, and physical unvirtuous deeds. Greed, hatred, and ignorance are the three unvirtuous deeds of the mind. Telling lies, divisive speech, harsh words, and gossip are the four unvirtuous deeds of speech. Killing, stealing, and sexual misconduct are the three unvirtuous deeds of the body.

According to Buddhism, the result of living a life filled with negative emotions and unvirtuous deeds is endless suffering in this life and rebirth in lower realms in the next. Nagarjuna explains:

By desire you take rebirth as a hungry ghost being.
By anger you are cast into a hell realm.
By ignorance, you go mostly to the animal realm.
By the opposite of these you take rebirth in the
    human or god realms.[157]

Even if we are able to take rebirth as a human again, if we have done negative deeds, it is certain that we will be tormented by the three sufferings: sufferings upon sufferings (one cause of pain piles up on another), sufferings of change (reversals of fortune), and all-pervasive sufferings (the inerent unsatisfactoriness of ordinary life).

So now is the time to recognize that the precious days and nights of our life are flying swiftly by, and that we are spending them mostly in idleness. If we keep to this course, we are bound to suffer in the future. So like a fashion model whose hair has caught fire, we must rouse ourselves from our torpor and rush to exert all our knowledge and power to forge ahead on the path of Dharma, which will liberate us from the pit of pain.

As beginners, we must dive into the spiritual journey by starting to train on the path of common teachings (Sutra). We must lay a strong foundation of a true spiritual life by following the ten virtuous deeds, which are refraining from the ten unvirtuous deeds. This will assure us happiness and peace in the future.

We must work directly on improving our minds by training in serious Dharma meditations that rely on the most powerful source of blessings, such as the Buddha of Loving-Kindness. We must sincerely pray to him with total devotion and receive the blessings of his loving-kindness. This way, our minds will become increasingly loving and kind.

Training in the Five Perfections

We must practice devotion and loving-kindness, which are the essence of the Six Perfections taught in Mahayana. The first five of these perfections are embodied in the first three Buddha Stages. They are:

1. Training in giving with *generosity*
2. Preserving *moral discipline*
3. Maintaining *patience*
4. Striving with *diligence* for virtuous deeds
5. Remaining in *contemplation* one-pointedly

Honing these five will enable us to reach the sixth perfection, *wisdom*, which is the essence of the Fourth Buddha Stage.

If we could do this, we will pacify the miseries that are caused by our own three poisonous thoughts and emotions. We will be sustained by the splendors of wholesomeness and happiness. We will accumulate merits and benefit others. After death, we will have the joy of rebirth in higher realms, even in manifested pure lands, such as the Blissful Pure Land of Amitabha Buddha.

Even if our meditation is not perfect, even if we don't transcend duality and emotion, our practice will still be beneficial. So when we're meditating on devotion, for instance, we might be grasping at the object of our devotion. But we will nevertheless be holding on to that object's virtuous aspects, which are ultimately sources of peace, joy, and openness. Even if, when we're meditating on loving-kindness, we have thoughts of clinging to positive deeds and happiness, those are still positive thoughts, and they'll help us and others. Whenever we do anything positive that is inspired by beneficial intentions, it will become a source of peace and joy.

So even though our ultimate goal may be to attain the Universal Buddha realizations that are free from grasping, to get there we need to start by developing a positive mindset and act accordingly.

It is by beginning with the Outer Buddha Stage, and the meditations that involve subjective-objective duality and concepts, that pure perception, devotion, loving-kindness, and wisdom will grow in us. Our step-by-step progress on this path will gradually loosen the tightness of our grip of grasping at self—"I" and "me," "this" and "that"—which is responsible for keeping us tightly bound in samsara. Our sense of contentment will grow and ease our wildfire-like attachment, desire, and lust. We will strengthen the force of our loving-kindness, pacifying our hurricanes of dislike, hatred, and anger. The brightness of wisdom will dispel the darkness of ignorance. The energies of devotion and trust in the Buddha and loving-kindness toward all beings will gradually blossom like flowers in sunlight. The thoughts of wishing joy for all beings boundlessly without conditions will awaken boundless openness, absolute peace, and limitless joy in us.

For a novice like me, there is no other way to enter the Dharma than by grasping on to virtuous objects and deeds at the beginning. Meditating on loving-kindness will initially be dualistic. But that's what enables us to start because that's where most of us beginners are. Remember, even if it is dual, it is still positive. And positive gradually leads to perfection, as we release the tightness of our mental grip of grasping and obsessions of our wants and needs. So meditations that start with positive dualistic grasping are indispensable to our eventually perfecting realization.

Amazing Devotees I Have Known

In Golok province of Eastern Tibet, where I was born and grew up, I knew many older laymen and laywomen who joyfully and vigorously prayed with unreserved devotion to the Buddha of Loving-Kindness and enjoyed heartfelt blessings.

Many of them were illiterate, in the Western sense. But in reality, they not only knew how to recite all the essential prayers and pray with true love for mother-beings and devotion to the Buddha, but they also did so sometimes more earnestly than many well-educated monks and nuns. Yet many of these laypeople knew very little about the fancy interpretations and complex meanings of the textual teachings. They weren't really interested in theoretical views of different traditions. Nor where they interested in becoming logicians who could criticize, defend, and refute intellectual and doctrinal arguments. They didn't care whether they could cite historical or bibliographical evidence. Most weren't interested in performing elaborate ceremonial liturgies.

But these laypeople had something that was far more precious: absolute trust, confidence, and devotion to the Buddha of Loving-Kindness and his unconditional love, as instructed by their teachers. They fully believed in his power to protect them from misfortune and fulfill all their needs if they prayed sincerely from their hearts. With this trust and devotion, they continuously recited the Six-Syllable Prayer as their daily spiritual prayer to the Buddha, day and night, unless they were asleep. While walking or sitting, even while eating and drinking, somewhere, somehow, the waves of devotional prayer were always alive on their breath. Even while they were asleep, if they woke up for a second or two in the night, I would hear them starting to recite their prayers a couple of times before they fell back asleep.

When I was growing up, I remember hearing from the father of my tutor Kyala Khenpo (Chechog Dondrub Tsal), whose name was Yumko of Kyala and who was then in his eighties, that when he was in bed, he held his prayer beads on his stomach as he was counting prayers instead of resting his hand on his bed. That way, he explained, the movements of the beads would keep him awake longer, so that he could say more prayers.

These wonderful devotees seem to have transformed the waves of their breath into a cycle of prayer, as if the chain of their thoughts was a continuous flow of devotion and all the waves of the phenomena around them turned into the presence and actions of the Buddha of Loving-Kindness, wishing joy for all.

That is why these older people, whether they were happy or in pain, rarely seemed to get distracted from the light of love of the Buddha. When they were happy, they would respect it as the blessings of Buddha's love. When they were sick or suffering, they would still maintain a sense of thankfulness by seeing it as a washing away of their negative deeds (karma) that, thanks to the power of the Buddha's unconditional care, they wouldn't have to experience in future. If they lived long, they used their years as an opportunity to pray more to their beloved Buddha and engage in more virtuous deeds for others. If they were dying, they would be pleased as if they were going home, since they fully trusted that the Buddha would lead them to his Pure Land—a Buddha paradise.

Because of the power and effects of these life-long positive thoughts and deeds, when the hour of their death arrived, most of these laypeople hardly felt sadness, pain or fear. While dying, many expressed joy at leaving for their long-awaited next destination, for which they had long prepared. They would start to describe their beautiful visions of Buddhas or Buddha pure lands and the soothing sounds of prayers.

According to the Buddhist teachings, when devout and meritorious meditators die, they behold clouds of enlightened ones such as the Buddha of Loving-Kindness in the sky before them, in the midst of lights of love with music and prayers. They move swiftly and peacefully through the bardo, the intermediate or transitional period between death and rebirth.[158] They take rebirth in a Buddha Pure Land of everlasting peace, joy, and wisdom.

In today's world, it is becoming harder and harder to

find people like this anywhere, inside or outside of Tibet. But when I was growing up, seeing people who led such meaningful lives opened my eyes to the world of true authentic teachings and meditators. These simple people became a great source of inner joy and true understanding for me. Whenever I think about them, I get lost in great wonder.

In case anyone is wondering, the dying visions of these laypeople were *not* hallucinations or delusions. They were the result of these people's transforming their mental habitual tendencies by pacifying conflicting and confused thoughts, healing bruised emotions, and cooling the flames of sensations. The kind of world or phenomena that people encounter after death is a manifestation of the qualities of their mind, of the habitual reflections they built over lifetimes. By the time death arrived, these laypeople were blossoming with the joyful energy of devotion and trust in the Buddha.

If our mind is full of devotion, trust, and loving-kindness, then what we will see and feel at death will be a world of ultimate joy and love. This transformation can take place in anyone, if they developed a mind of true trust and devotion to the Buddha of Loving-Kindness and if they prayed with the skillful means of devotion from the core of the heart.

Some people might question whether these laypeople's experiences were unreal or the result of self-brainwashing. My reply is that, if so, their minds were washed—not by the customary torrent of greed, hatred, and jealousy—but by the blessing stream of loving-kindness, peace, and joy. I would choose the latter over the former any day.

I would like to add that I have also seen strongly religious devotees, lay and ordained, of non-Buddhist religious traditions. They lived a simple life, content with little; developed enduring faith in the Blessed Ones, the objects of their beliefs; and had strong loving-kindness and compassion for others. Many amazing individuals spend their lives and resources to protect and educate others and serve their essential needs. They pursue no or very few personal mundane gains for themselves. They have often been inspired to their spiritual vocation by some extraordinary teaching or individual who is devoted to loving-kindness, compassion, and trust, just as the Buddha and Buddhist teachings inspire Buddhists.

Training in the Sixth Perfection

Once you gain accomplishments in the first three Buddha Stages, you can more confidently accomplish the meditation on wisdom, the Sixth Perfection, which is the essence of the fourth Buddha Stage. Accomplished meditators realize the profound wisdom of the two truths—relative truth through the first five perfections and absolute truth through the sixth perfection. Nagarjuna writes:

> The teachings that are taught by the Buddhas
> Are fully based on the two truths:
> The relative truth of the mundane world
> And the absolute truth of the holy Dharma.
> Those who do not know perfectly
> The divisions of the two truths
> Will not know the profound truth

Of the teachings of the Buddha.
Without relying on conventional truth,
The absolute meaning cannot be taught.
Without realizing the meaning of absolute truth,
Nirvana will not be attained.[159]

Accomplished meditators train in the views and meditations taught in the high teachings of Mahayana, such as Madhyamaka, Tantra, Mahamudra, and Dzogpa Chenpo. They thereby realize the union of boundless loving-kindness and profound emptiness wisdom—that is, the selflessness or non-existence of what are known as the "three aspects": subject, agent, and action. That is loving-kindness free from concepts.

As the ultimate result, these practitioners will attain supreme Buddhahood with the fourfold enlightened bodies and fivefold wisdoms that go beyond the extremes of falling into the suffering of samsara or the mere peace of nirvana. They will enjoy the power of spontaneously fulfilling the needs of infinite beings, whoever may be open to it, while remaining in the absolute nature.

However, most of us, like me, are still beginners even though we have been meditating for a while. The problem is that we haven't fully and openly dedicated our mind to it or sincerely and fully blended with our meditation experiences. So until we make real progress in the meditations that we are doing, we must focus on common, elementary meditation trainings—generating positive thoughts and feelings, as in the Outer Buddha Stage. Though dualistic and emotional, these foundational trainings on positive concepts are suitable for us and will help us establish a base of heartfelt spiritual energy. Once these elementary meditation experiences become clearer, deeper, and more stable, we may move to higher stages with ease.

There are many whose minds are still ordinary in that they can hold rigid dualistic concepts and emotions like hatred and greed. Yet some of these practitioners claim to be adepts of wisdom free from concepts, as taught in the highest teachings in Tantra, Mahamudra, and Dzogpa Chenpo. However, being intellectually proficient in the texts of the highest teachings without any real realization does not make one an adept or qualify one to instruct others in those fields.

Meditators of Neutral States

In the West, there are many who approach Buddhism primarily intellectually. In the East, many approach it primarily as a tradition—part of their cultural heritage. Yes, Buddhism contains immensely profound and complex intellectual information. Yes, it is an important cultural tradition in many Eastern civilizations. However, Buddhism's true gift is that it teaches us to learn and experience the true characteristics and the nature of our mind and the world, as they are. Through meditations like those on loving-kindness, compassion, devotion, and wisdom, Buddhism trains us to improve our mind in how we think, communicate, and act with others and the external world. If our mind becomes wholesome, then our vocal and physical activities will become sources of peace and benefit for ourselves and others. This life will be happier, as will the next. Ultimately, through proper meditation, we will be liberated from the suffering of samsara.

No matter how much we study the texts, we need to be mindful of our karma in order to progress. We must stay away from unvirtuous acts and thoughts. But we shouldn't fritter away our lives by engaging only in neutral karmas. Instead, we should exert ourselves in virtuous karmas such as prayer and service.

Some meditators choose to remain in the absence of awareness. In my experience, these are usually well-educated, high-status achievers. They are often so busy burning both ends of the candle in order to advance their worldly position that they even dream about earning at night. So, understandably, they feel a tremendous sense of relief when someone instructs them, "Just rest in the absence of thoughts." At last, they can quiet down and let go of their busyness! And since the instruction to do so is given to them by someone whom they consider to be an authority on meditation, they don't have to feel guilty about slowing down. They are told that doing this is good for their health and mental state. So for these fatigued individuals, having permission to rest without thoughts is new and exciting, something they have rarely tasted.

In reality, however, this meditation experience is a neutral state. Most of these people are simply taking a break while still in the middle of mundane traffic, still in the hub of ordinary karmic and mental habitual settings—without having purified, refined, or transcended their mental and emotional afflictions. So when they come out of that break, that trance, they find themselves back at square one, with the same old mundane dilemmas and habits awaiting them. It is like waking up from a wonderful dream only to find oneself back in reality.

Nevertheless, remaining in neutral thoughts and activities is better than spending one's life in evil thoughts and deeds, which will cause grave pain. However, spending one's life in a neutral state is a big waste of the great potential of our most precious human life.

According to Buddhist teachings, the karmic result of remaining in a neutral state, the mere absence of thoughts, is rebirth in the animal, form or formless realms. We go to the animal realm if our mental habit was ignorance and stupidity. This realm is marked by violence and fear.

We take rebirth in the formless realms if our habitual thought patterns were marked by ideas like "Space is infinite," "Consciousness is infinite," "There is nothing," or "There is no perception and no absence of perception." Each of these four thought patterns leads to rebirth in a different subdivision of the formless realms, depending on which subdivision best reflects our habits. For instance, having a habit of thinking "Space is infinite" lands us in the subdivision called "infinite space."[160] In the formless realm, we don't have gross bodies or forms. We don't have gross thoughts or emotions. This is due to the past experience of remaining in the absence of thoughts and absence of awareness.

Absorption in the formless realm can last for eons. Eventually, however, it ends. And when it does, we continue from where we left off—returning to our old thoughts and emotions, and experiencing the results of our other positive or negative past karmas. So taking rebirth in the formless realms is a break, a limbo, but with no merits. It is a diversion from the path of liberation, as there is no awakening of the wisdom of intrinsic awareness or discriminative wisdom. That is why Longchen Rabjam laments for those meditators who value remaining in the absence of thoughts:

> Alas! These animal-like meditators,
> By stopping the perceptions, they remain without any thought.
> Calling this the absolute nature, they become proud.
> If they gain experience in such a state, they will take rebirth in the animal realm.
> Even if they don't gain much experience in it, they will take rebirth in the form or formless realms.
> They will have no opportunity to get liberation from samsara.[161]

As long as we make no effort to transform the mind, we cannot escape the ordinary state of grasping tightly at mental objects—dualistically, emotionally, and sensorily. A merely neutral state in which concepts are temporarily suspended won't help us progress. As soon as we go back to having concepts again, we will return to the ordinary state of grasping we had before. It is like waking up from the escapism of deep sleep, only to find that the same mundane problems await us. Kamalashila[162] writes:

> The assertion "not thinking anything" is a denial of wisdom, the very characteristic of pure discernment. Since the root of pure wisdom is pure discernment, if you reject discernment you are abandoning the wisdom that transcends samsara, as you have cut it from the root.[163]

Kamalashila emphasizes the need for discernment in order to realize wisdom—and cut through self-delusion:

> You must understand the holy Dharma teachings about freedom from recollections and freedom from thoughts in the mind. However, these must be preceded by pure discernment because [only] pure discernment frees you from recollections and thoughts; nothing else does.[164]

Meditators under Self-Delusion

Then there are other meditators who believe or act as though they have attained high goals, but whose meditations haven't really penetrated their minds. Yukhog Chatralwa, a great meditation Master whom I knew in my youth, quoted the following:

> Yidzhin Dzodgrel Padma Karpo says, "These days, [there are those whose mundane] mind and mental events remain untouched no matter what. They have not yet purified their feelings of happiness and unhappiness or the waves of their breathing. Yet they claim to remain in the state of Buddha realization. I promise you—since they haven't even accomplished any worldly absorption—there is no way they could have transcended the mundane world."[165]

The right way to avoid the risk of falling into a neutral state or self-delusion is to earnestly follow the step-by-step sequence of practices on generating virtuous deeds through the Outer, Inner, and Universal Buddha Stages and awakening of wisdom through the Ultimate Buddha Stage.

12

DEDICATIONS AND ASPIRATIONS

DEDICATION AND ASPIRATION are among the greatest skillful means to multiply the power of meditations. As soon as you complete the Four Buddha Stages, you should lovingly and joyfully dedicate, or give away, your merits to all mother-beings for their happiness now and for their ultimate enlightenment. Dedicate all the merits that you just accumulated in your practice, that you accumulated in the past, and that you will accumulate.

If dedicating your merits is like giving away seeds to others, then making aspirations is like causing the seeds to ripen in a particular way. You should make aspirations, thinking and saying:

> By the power of the virtuous deeds that we have dedicated as the cause of happiness and enlightenment for all, may all beings' positive wishes, whatever they are, be fulfilled and may all attain enlightenment, as the result.

Dedication and aspiration are not ancillary to practice. They are an integral part of the main body of training.

Dedicating merits and making aspirations have many benefits, according to Buddhism. First, they almost

miraculously increase the power of the merits of the virtuous deeds that we dedicated. The more we dedicate and
make aspirations with loving-kindness in our heart, the
better we serve those whom we are trying to reach with
our dedication. The more we benefit others, the more we
ourselves benefit.

Second, dedicating and making aspirations protect
the merits from being destroyed by any subsequent unvirtuous deeds or thoughts that we may engage in.

In fact, dedicating and making aspirations are such an
important part of practice that we don't necessarily need to
wait until the end of our meditation session. We can dedicate and aspire every now and then, during the meditation;
and we must at least briefly dedicate and aspire whenever
we take a short break.

No matter how brief our thought of loving-kindness—
even if we utter only a single mantra with devotion—we
should dedicate it as the cause of boundless benefits for infinite mother-beings and rejoice over it. If we could feel joy
that we meditated and dedicated it for a golden aspiration,
such as serving boundless mother-beings, that will greatly
increase the power and quantity of our merits, just as pouring oil on a fire magnifies the blaze. Even if our virtuous
deed seems small, if we repeatedly rejoice inwardly over it
for days or weeks on end, the merits of this deed will continue to grow like the Mississippi River in the summer, and
may even become inexhaustible.

13

BENEFITS OF LOVING-KINDNESS MEDITATION

IT'S HARD TO FATHOM THE BENEFITS for ourselves and others of doing loving-kindness meditations. First, the merits produced by meditating on loving-kindness are virtually inconceivable. They are greater than many other, even highly meritorious trainings. Consider what some of the greatest Masters and scriptures, of Tantra and Sutra, have said about the merits produced by loving-kindness training, starting with the Buddha himself, who said:

> The [merits of] making all kinds of offerings
> To the sublime beings [Buddhas]
> In the millions and billions of pure lands
> Cannot compare with [the merits of]
> One thought of loving-kindness.[166]

The Buddha also said:

> O Child of Good Family! The merits of generating loving-kindness for the time it takes to snap one's fingers in this world is much greater than [the

merits] of observing ascetic discipline for hundreds of thousands of years in [the Buddha Pure Land known as] "Adorned by a Thousand Worlds."[167]

When the thought of loving-kindness is multiplied so that it extends to boundless beings, the merits produced are inexhaustible. The *Lodrö Mizepe Tenpa* sutra records the following dialogue between Shariputra, one of the Buddha's chief disciples, and another disciple, Lodrö Mizepa:

[Lodrö Mizepa:] O Shariputra, beings are limitless and the loving-kindness of the bodhisattvas pervades all. O Ascetic Shariputra, do you think the immeasurable meritorious roots that the bodhisattvas created can be exhausted?

Answer: O Son of Good Family, they cannot be exhausted. Whoever thinks that the merits of loving-kindness can be exhausted must obviously believe that space is finite![168]

Further, if we practice loving-kindness—or any meditation, for that matter—while we are facing difficulties or undergoing hardships, then that will make our merits all the greater.

Second, loving-kindness purifies our negative emotions. The Buddha said:

Whoever is sure of falling into the three inferior realms
Due to having committed verbal and physical
    misdeeds
Will be purified by loving-kindness.[169]

A tantra also says:

> Loving-kindness purifies anger into its own state.
> It perfects mirror-like wisdom.[170]

Third, loving-kindness is therefore our best defense against adversity—because it purifies the negative emotions that create negative karma. Je Tsongkhapa writes that loving-kindness "is the best protection for you—the Buddha tamed demons through the power of his loving-kindness."[171]

Fourth, meditations on loving-kindness give us the strength, confidence, and skill to take both the happiness and suffering of our lives as the path to enlightenment. They teach us to take whatever we see, hear, and feel as the means and expression of loving-kindness in various forms.

Some Specific Benefits

Meditators of loving-kindness receive many other specific benefits, too. The Buddha enumerated eleven:

> I will teach you eleven benefits. What are the eleven benefits? They sleep comfortably and wake up comfortably. They will not have un-virtuous dreams. People adore them. Nonhuman beings adore them. Gods protect them. They will not be harmed by fire, poison, or weapons. Their minds will always be joyful. Their faces will be clear. Their minds will be at peace when they die. They

will be reborn in celestial realms because of their mindfulness [of morality].[172]

Nagarjuna also lists the benefits of loving-kindness:

> Celestial beings and humans will be kind to you.
> They will protect you.
> You will enjoy a happy mind and much more
>   happiness.
> You will not be harmed by poison or weapons.
> You will achieve your goals without effort.
> You will take rebirth in the celestial realms.
> Even if you could not attain liberation,
> You will enjoy these eight benefits [as the result of]
>   loving-kindness.[173]

Je Tsongkhapa also noted:

> If you have loving-kindness, celestial and human beings will adore you. They will come to you effortlessly.[174]

Loving-Kindness Leads Us to Buddhahood via the Two Accumulations

By successfully completing the training on loving-kindness, we will realize all the accomplishments of the Mahayana path with its two levels of bodhichitta. Generating the thought of wishing joy and enlightenment for all is the practice of *aspirational bodhichitta*. Actually implementing that thought by training in the Six Perfections is *engaged bodhichitta:*

1. The aspect of opening our heart of loving-kindness widely for all is giving, or *generosity.*
2. Preserving loving-kindness without letting it be stained by negative thoughts, emotions, or acts is *discipline.*
3. Remaining in loving-kindness by tolerating any hardship is *patience.*
4. Exerting ourselves in loving-kindness with great enthusiasm without letting ourselves be swayed by laziness is *diligence.*
5. Dwelling in loving-kindness without distraction is *contemplation.*
6. Seeing and realizing the different stages of loving-kindness as they are, particularly loving-kindness free from concepts, is *wisdom.*

LOVING-KINDNESS ACCOMPLISHES THE TWO ACCUMULATIONS VIA THE SIX PERFECTIONS

Loving-kindness meditations lead us to Buddhahood through the "two accumulations"—of merits and of wisdom. We need both accumulations to become a Buddha. The first five of the Six Perfections are the accumulation of merits. The sixth perfection—the perfection of wisdom—is the accumulation of wisdom.

By accumulating merits, we attain the "form bodies" of Buddhahood with which to serve others. By accumulating wisdom, we attain the "ultimate body" of Buddhahood, free from inherent and transitory obscurations. Nagarjuna writes:

> The form bodies of the Buddhas
> Are generated from the accumulation of merits.
> The ultimate body
> Is generated from the accumulation of wisdom.[175]

Loving-kindness is, in short, the most profound training that exists. As Karma Chagme says:

> To develop loving-kindness and compassion is to develop bodhichitta. There is no training more profound than these in either the sutras or tantras. Please do not be lax in practicing them.[176]

PART THREE

LOVING-KINDNESS
IN DAILY LIFE

14

HEALING PHYSICAL
AND MENTAL ILLS

THE POWER OF OUR DEVOTION to the Buddha and our unconditional love toward all heal our life's mental, physical, and karmic ills; reduce our stress, confusion, and pain; make the power of our heartfelt loving-kindness blossom; and awaken the enlightened nature of our mind. In many sutras and tantras, thinking or praying to the Buddha of Loving-Kindness from the heart is recommended as the key to pacifying and healing illness and fear.

Healing Physical Ills

The Buddha said:

> If you remember the Lord Avalokiteshvara . . .
> The torments of birth, old-age, and sickness will be
>   pacified.[177]

When I was growing up in Tibet, sick people generally went first to a Lama and then to the doctor for medicine. That wasn't just because of the culture, but because it seemed that prayers healed more effectively than medicines. We believed that prayer addressed the karmic disorders that are the roots of disease. Many people were visibly healed through prayer and meditation, including on loving-kindness.

You can use the following loving-kindness meditation to help heal physical sicknesses, yours and others', by yourself. Loving-kindness is the most powerful healing meditation. So if you can do it by yourself effectively, you will be your own most effective healer. If you are working with a patient, visualize the patient, as well as yourself, going through the healing meditation.

VISUALIZATION FOR PHYSICAL HEALING

Begin by visualizing the Buddha of Loving-Kindness sitting in space before you as the source of healing blessings. Believe from the depth of your heart that he is the embodiment of the wisdom, love, and power of all the enlightened ones, and that he has the power to heal all diseases with their causes.

Then pray with devotion and trust in the Buddha and his power from the depth of your heart by singing or reciting, aloud or silently, the sacred Six-Syllable Prayer hundreds and thousands of times to heal all the sickness in the world, or the sickness of a particular person with its causes and conditions.

Think and feel that your mind is fully open to the Buddha with the energy of devotion and trust and to his healing power and the prayers. Then, from the Buddha's body, visualize that the healing power of his omniscient wisdom, unconditional love, and boundless power is radiating in the form of bright and colorful light (or blessing nectar of light) with blissful heat energy. Those beams of blessing light are infused with the energy force of his loving-kindness, his wish for joy for all beings. Those lights enter your body and suffuse it from head to toe.

Visualize that all your diseases with their causes are in the form of darkness in your body, wherever they may be located, and feel them. Then visualize and feel that every particle of your body is fully filled by the Buddha's blessing light of unconditional love.

All the diseases in the form of darkness are slowly but completely dispelled and purified without leaving a trace behind, like the clearing of darkness on the earth by the sun's bright daylight.

Repeat this exercise many times and enjoy the feeling of being free from the disease.

Then repeatedly think and feel that every particle of your body is filled with the blessing lights of wisdom, love, and power with blissful energies of the Buddha. Every particle is transformed into boundless particles of blessing light with blazing blissful heat. Every particle of your body is breathing—exhaling and inhaling—the blissful heat energy waves of loving-kindness with sounds of the Six-Syllable Mantra. Repeat this many times.

If you are a beginner, take extra time to focus your mental and physical energies on whatever meditation you are doing, and try to relax or open fully and boundlessly. Repeating the same meditation over and over helps activate, strengthen, and concentrate the energies of mind and body. It also makes them open, peaceful, and expansive, just as repeatedly tightening and relaxing the muscles during exercise strengthens them and expands the body's energy.

As you enjoy the healing process of your physical body, you are also healing your mental ailments, since the mind is the one experiencing the power of the healing process of the body.

VISUALIZING NECTAR OF LIGHT

You could also use nectar of light as the healing agent. If you prefer that, then visualize and feel that from the body of the Buddha of Loving-Kindness, his wisdom, love, and power pour forth in the form of a blessing stream of nectar of light that floods down into you through the force of his loving-kindness.

All your sicknesses and their causes are in the form of filth, blood, and pus in your body. The stream of nectar fully fills your body's every particle. All the filth is completely washed away by the powerful stream of nectar, like dirt washed from a vessel. All the impurities pour out through the lower doors and pores of your body. Not even a trace of dirt is left.

Or you could think that the blissful heat of the nectar stream melts all the tumors of your body, as hot water melts snowflakes or sunlight melts frost—simply by touching them. The residues of the tumors then exit your body without remainder. All the ill effects of toxins and harmful organisms are washed out by the force of the flow of nectar, without leaving a speck behind. All the diseases caused by the imbalances in the elements and temperature of the body are dissolved and washed away in the form of impurities. All injuries caused by evil forces are expelled in the form of blood, pus, and phlegm. All evil deeds and evil habits that you have been harboring are washed out in the form of smoke and silt.

At the end, the impurities that are washed out of your body amass in outer space, where they dissolve and evaporate into the emptiness of space, without leaving any trace, like water evaporating in the summer heat or clouds fading away into the sky.

Your body is now clean, pure, healthy, translucent, and glowing with pure light, filled with the feeling of blissful heat and power. Your body has transformed into a body of blessing nectar of light—light of wisdom, love, and power—with incredible blissful heat.

Finally, when you are ready, rest in the state of the union of loving-kindness and openness—that is, the loving-kindness that is free from concepts. In that state, there is no subjective or objective duality, no positive or negative thoughts, no attachment or hate, and no joyful or painful sensations. Or at least, just rest in greater peace, as much as you can.

The power of your meditation, with devotion in the Buddha and his unconditional love, heals your mental, physical, and karmic ills. It frees you from mental stress, confusion, and anguish. It allows the power of your heartfelt loving-kindness to blossom. And it awakens the enlightened nature of your mind.

Healing Mental Ills

Mental and emotional issues are generally very responsive to loving-kindness meditations if we are open to them.

In life, everyone encounters mental and emotional

pain. According to Buddhism, the root source of these challenges, as with everything we experience, is the mind. Our mental and emotional pain is rooted in our mind's grasping at this or that. Our mind grasps because we do not realize that these objects and experiences are not objectively real, as we believe they are. Rather, they are projections and designations of our mind. That is why the more we entertain anxiety, the more our mental ills increase. Shantideva writes: "People who harbor anxiety will face more problems."[178]

Yet it is precisely because emotional pain and unhappiness are created by and experienced by the mind that they can also be healed by the mind. We can eliminate many emotional or mental issues through prayer and meditation. The important thing is to use the emotional obstacles we face to awaken and deepen spiritual qualities like devotion and loving-kindness and to learn to apply these qualities to minimize, eliminate, or even welcome challenges so that they become a support in our life's spiritual journey.

Meditation to Heal Emotional Problems

Let us start with a guided meditation to heal emotional problems, your own or others'. If you are trying to help someone else, you can visualize them and yourself doing the meditation.

Begin by developing trust from the depth of the heart in the Buddha of Loving-Kindness's omniscient wisdom, unconditional love for all, and boundless power to heal mental suffering with its causes and conditions.

Pray to the Buddha with great devotion from the heart

to pacify and heal all your mental suffering with their causes—as many times as you can.

Then visualize and feel that from the Buddha's body come the blessings of his body, speech, and mind and the blessings of his omniscient wisdom, unconditional love, and boundless power to heal you. The blessings are in the form of beams of light with powerful blissful heat. Every particle of your body is fully filled by the bright blessing lights. Let them ease your mind. Just rest in them for a while.

Visualize that your mental pain with its causes are in the form of darkness in your body. See and feel them for a while.

Then see that the brightness and warmth of the Buddha's blessing lights enter you, thanks to the power of your devotion to the Buddha and the power of his unconditional love. See that the lights fully dispel and purify that darkness from your physical body, energy cycle, and mindstream.

Keep enjoying the incredible blissful heat of the bright blessing lights. Take time to sunbathe in the warmth of the Buddha's light of unconditional love. Feel that any feelings of sadness, pain, and fear dissolve in the total security and warmth of the Buddha's loving-kindness, like a child finally reunited with his or her loving parents. Soak in the feeling of being unconditionally loved, as if taking a long, warm bath. Try to rest in that without letting your mind wander. Inhale and exhale as the waves of the energies of happiness and joy expand from your heart with the sound of the Six-Syllable Mantra, recited aloud or silently.

Think with your mind, feel in your body, and trust in

your heart that your body and mind are purified—not in some vague, generic, superficial way, but deeply and thoroughly in detail. Every particle of your body and every aspect of your mind has been purified and transformed into a stream of joyful thoughts and radiant light—the light of wisdom, love, and power of the Buddha with blissful heat brought by the boundless loving energy waves of the Buddha of Loving-Kindness.

THE HEALING BENEFITS OF THIS MEDITATION

This meditation can totally pacify and purify your suffering without leaving any trace and replace it with the enormous wealth of virtues of loving-kindness. This is due to the power of the Buddha's healing blessings, your virtuous thoughts in general, and your meditation on loving-kindness in particular.

The words of the Third Dodrupchen below, although he is speaking about compassion, apply equally to loving-kindness. The qualities and benefits of compassion and loving-kindness are, after all, the same. The Third Dodrupchen says:

> In the Abhidharma[179] it is said that "illness is the maturation of a violent deed, while compassion is an action totally free from violence." That is why the Buddha of Compassion [and Loving-Kindness] is the supreme deity [for healing]. Precisely because of these points, it is said that Jowo [Atisha][180] was renowned for "his greatness in healing illness due to his having abandoned violence."[181]

Recognize, appreciate, and enjoy the feeling that your suffering has been transformed into peace, joy, and strength, or whatever improvement you made, big or small.

ADDITIONAL WAYS TO HANDLE MENTAL AND EMOTIONAL CHALLENGES

In addition to this meditation, if you are able, there are a number of other ways in which to work with mental and emotional suffering and turn it into a support for our spiritual path.

1. *Acceptance.* When some person or situation causes us pain, sadness or fear, our usual reaction is to blame them and get angry at them. Instead, try to accept the problem gracefully, as it is the result of your own past karma. Take it as the blessing of the Buddha: by experiencing it now, you will later be free from that negative karmic debt and have a brighter future. This understanding helps heal you since, by welcoming suffering with a positive mind-set and seeing it as the Buddha's blessing, you are purifying your negative karmas.

2. *Endurance.* Instead of focusing on healing your own pain, think and wish that the pain of all beings merges into your pain and that you are enduring the pain so that they won't have to endure it. Then tolerate it on behalf of all beings with loving-kindness. This meditation helps heal suffering through the power of loving-kindness and illness.

3. *Rest in openness.* Rather than trying to eliminate the pain, look at the true nature of the pain itself and rest in it without modifications. To be able to do this effectively, you need to be well trained in the experience of

the ultimate nature, such as taught in the Ultimate Buddha Stage. When you look at the pain with openness, you can enjoy the awareness of the openness nature. So the true nature of the pain and the nature of your mind unite as the realization of ultimate wisdom. Then dualistic mental concepts, the root of pain and suffering, dissolve into the ultimate state.

TURNING HAPPINESS AND SUFFERING INTO THE PATH OF ENLIGHTENMENT

The above three methods can be found in a wonderful article by the Third Dodrupchen Rinpoche called "Turning Happiness and Suffering into the Path of Enlightenment."[182] The article is unique—short yet profound, with much advice that is highly relevant to today's readers, whether lay or ordained. It teaches how to transform suffering—and happiness as well—into the path of peace and enlightenment.

As the Third Dodrupchen writes elsewhere, there are three possible levels of meditative strength and realization:

> There are the superior, intermediate, and lesser ways of taking illness as the path. The superior way is to rest your mind in the [nature of the] severe pain without making any alterations. Then the nature of the illness—emptiness that is free from elaborations—will arise.
>
> The intermediate way is to bring all the illnesses and ill effects of all beings together in your

severe pain and take that pain as the path [of meditation]. The pain and its emotional [causes] will cease because the pain becomes the support for virtuous deeds.

The lesser way is to recognize that sicknesses are your past karmic debts. Don't make efforts to heal them or turn them into objects of resentment. Instead, see them as occurring by the kindness of the Precious Jewels [Buddha, Dharma, and Sangha]. Then the effects [or debts] of those past evil deeds [which are the causes of sickness] will be purified.[183]

Whatever obstacles we experience, if we can take them the right way, they won't obstruct our spiritual path. Rather, they will become a tool to stimulate our advancement toward our destination: unconditional love and enlightenment.

So try to feel joy when facing difficulties, for they provide the chance to purify unvirtuous past deeds, the cause of ills, and infuse us with the inspiration to generate yet greater virtuous deeds, the cause of healing and enlightenment.

If your mental and emotional problems could become an inspiration for your spiritual progress, make a point to recognize them as such. That recognition will, in turn, fuel joy and inspiration in your mind. If you nurture and strengthen that joy by enjoying it again and again, you unleash the true healing energy of joy. With that, you can prevent anything from turning into an obstacle. But this is not just about averting challenges so they don't harm you. It is about transmuting problems so that they fuel your healing momentum. The Third Dodrupchen writes:

> The meaning of not getting hurt by obstacles is not that obstacles like illness could be reversed or averted from taking place in the future, but that they will not be able to obstruct your accomplishments on the path. To achieve this goal, you must nurture two kinds of attitudes: stop the attitude of totally not wanting suffering, and develop the attitude of liking suffering. . . . Also, it is not good enough simply to use the arising of suffering as a support for virtuous deeds. It is definitely necessary that you also train your mind to have a strong and durable feeling of joy that has been inspired by recognizing the transformations that have taken place [in you].[184]

15

DEALING WITH CHALLENGING PEOPLE

THERE ARE THREE WAYS to deal with challenging people, as advised in the teachings of Buddhism.

1. The ordinary and simplest way is to avoid the person with whom you have a problem—whether, for instance, a harsh person who makes you angry or an attractive person to whom you are getting overly attached. Shift the focus of your mind to something helpful or unrelated, such as friends, flowers, music, or nature. If you don't give the person attention, your mind will be free of them. If the person is trying to hurt or provoke you, and if you do not respond, you neutralize them and they may become helpless in trying to inflict harm and provoke you. They may give up and even change their attitude toward you.

The strategy of avoiding helps you as well as them. It saves you from being hurt by this person and saves the person from getting further into the habit of creating bad karmas.

2. The intermediate way is to eliminate or pacify your negative emotions toward this person by applying a powerful antidote. Pure loving-kindness and compassion are antidotes to all negative emotions. Chapter 4 details how to

generate unconditional love by seeing even "foes" as your kind mother.

3. The highest but most difficult way is to transform your anger, attachment, or other negative mental state into wisdom. If you have had any experience in meditation on the wisdom of loving-kindness that is free from concepts, as detailed in the Ultimate Buddha Stage (see chapter 9), you should use that. That will be the most effective way to deal with challenging people.

I'd like to add that, in dealing with difficult people, it is important to be guided, not necessarily by what you would like, but by what will be most beneficial to you, them, and others. That is how to best help the person you are dealing with as well as people at large.

If you cannot resolve the issue in a loving, gentle way, then harsh and wrathful words or actions may be necessary if they will be beneficial. Atisha says:

> The supreme teachers are those who confront your hidden faults.
> The supreme instructions are those that deal with your faults.[185]

However, if you use harsh expressions, be sure that they come out of a peaceful mind and loving heart that wants to help others, like "tough love" or like the wrathful Buddhas. Wrathful expressions must never come out of selfish intentions or negative emotions, such as wanting to hurt another. Patrul Rinpoche writes: "There are times when the bodhisattvas are allowed to commit the seven unvirtuous deeds of body and speech, as long as their minds are pure and free from selfish intention."[186]

If harsh words or acts come out of negative emotions, they become evil deeds, which will mostly hurt others and definitely oneself. So refrain from expressing them at all costs. If you feel yourself burning with the urge to say or do something negative, just be quiet. As Shantideva writes:

> When your mind wishes to get attached
> Or get angry,
> At that time, don't say or do anything.
> Remain like a log.[187]

So we must remember that the Buddha of Loving-Kindness is present in all that we see, hear, and feel—even in the ugliest, harshest beings. If we are skilled and open, we will see the loving-kindness of the Buddha everywhere, like the sun rays shining through even the thickest, darkest clouds. Seeing, hearing, and enjoying all beings in the qualities of Buddha's love, pray: OM MA-NI PAD-ME HUNG.

16

Daily Activities as Training in Loving-Kindness

We should make an effort not to leave our practice behind on our cushion or in some weekend meditation hall. Our daily activities during off-meditation periods present many chances for us to continue to pursue the right path and make progress on it. We should try to maintain thoughts and feelings of loving-kindness in our mind and turn all our activities into loving-kindness in action, or at least make sure that our activities are supportive of, not destructive of, loving-kindness.

If we don't know how to do this, or don't try to, we will lose many great opportunities. Unhelpful daily activities could even pull us away from the spiritual experiences that we earned during our meditation sessions. So, with thoughts of loving-kindness, we must try to turn all our daily activities into bodhisattva activities with great enthusiasm.

During off-meditation periods, whatever our activity —such as cleaning, gardening, cooking, driving, washing, talking, or resting—we could combine it with the thoughts and feelings of the amazing aspirations of loving-kindness as the basis and engage in any wholesome work with the efforts of the Six Perfections to try to make the activity fully healthy, pure, effective, and beneficial for all or many.

For example, if you are going to do gardening, first meditate on the Buddha of Loving-Kindness briefly with strong devotion. Develop the thought and feeling of loving-kindness in your heart, as you have learned to do earlier in this book. With the thought of loving-kindness in your heart, work on gardening with the Six Perfections.

Training in the Six Perfections can be explained in many ways, but for our purposes here they are as follows.

1. When you garden (or do any daily activity), imagine that you are doing it to bring joy to infinite beings, visible and invisible. Do it for them without attachment. Then it becomes the perfection of *generosity*.
2. Be the best gardener you can be, while staying peaceful. That is *discipline*.
3. Happily put up with any challenges, while staying calm and humble. That is *patience*.
4. Give your time, energy, and skill wholeheartedly and joyfully to the gardening, while being able to let go. That is *diligence*.
5. Focus on your gardening calmly and fully, remaining in the loving-kindness nature of the mind. That is *contemplation*.
6. Garden with full awareness with no—or with less—grasping at this or that. That is *wisdom*.

When you finish, mentally dedicate the merits from your gardening work and meditation to all mother-beings as the cause of their happiness and enlightenment. Then gardening will become a powerful training in the aspiration of loving-kindness, as well as in loving-kindness in action. Training in loving-kindness with the Six Perfections is the most important path of training for enlightenment, according to Mahayana teachings.

Jowoje Atisha explains the essential meaning of the Six Perfections:

> Not having attachment is the supreme among giving.
> Keeping the mind peaceful is the supreme among discipline.
> Remaining humble is the supreme among patience.
> Letting go of all activities is the supreme among diligence.
> Not altering the mind is the supreme among contemplation.
> Not grasping at [any object] is the supreme among wisdom.[188]

Most importantly, if our mind is not separated from thoughts of loving-kindness, whatever we are thinking will become thoughts of loving-kindness, the precious bodhichitta. Then whatever we say and do will become the expression of loving-kindness, causing only happiness and benefit to others and oneself. If that happens, due to the power of such skillful means, all our daily mental, vocal, and physical activities will, like the natural flow of a stream, spontaneously turn into the activities of Six Perfections of the bodhisattva path. Every activity of our life will become, directly or indirectly, the cause of accomplishing the two accumulations—of merits and of wisdom.

For beginners, however, it is important to stay away from people and objects that attract our minds in unwholesome directions. Whether we like to admit it or not, we are highly impressionable, since neither our minds nor our realizations are yet firm or strong. So we must always be alert about what we are feeding ourselves and what is happening before we associate with anything too closely. Ngulchu Thogme writes:

> Whomever you associate with, if they cause an
>   increase in your three poisons,
> A decline in your studying, pondering, and
>   meditating, or
> The disappearance of your loving-kindness and
>   compassion,
> Then you must renounce such evil friends. This is the
>   practice of bodhisattvas.[189]

Although spending our life serving others is the ideal for a bodhisattva trainee, in our extremely rushed modern lives, instead of helping anyone, we could easily be dragged into unwholesome thoughts and actions by associating with unwholesome people or situations. If that is a possibility, staying away is the best solution. That is why the great Jowoje Atisha gave the following advice:

> This degenerate age is not the time for bragging, but for hard work. It is not the time for holding high positions, but for low posts. It is not the time

for having servants, but for solitude. It is not the time to be concerned about having disciples, but about improving oneself. It is not the time to focus on words, but on meaning. It is not the time for traveling, but for staying put.[190]

Some Important Points for Daily Life

While meditating on loving-kindness, there are a number of points to keep in mind.

First, whenever we witness suffering or think of someone who is in pain, we must immediately meditate on compassion. We should think and feel over and over: "May the suffering that this being and many others are experiencing cease, along with its causes. I will do everything I can to free them from this pain."

Second, we should pay extra-special attention to those who are particularly kind to us or close to us, and who are seriously suffering. Patrul Rinpoche writes:

Especially, if you serve those who are your parents or those who are sick for a long time through your three doors, the merits will be immeasurable.
The sublime Jowoje [Atisha] said:

"If you generate loving-kindness to travelers from a long distance, those who are chronically ill and your old and fragile parents, the [merits of such practice] will be comparable to [the merits of] doing [high] meditations on emptiness with the essence of compassion."[191]

Daily Activities as Training in Loving-Kindness · 187

Third, it is usually easy to wish joy and enlightenment to people whom we like and care about, like friends and family, or to those we find attractive. But it is in these cases that we need to be especially careful to keep our meditation pure, or we could wind up strengthening attachment. If we do, our grip of grasping at "self" will become tighter; our intentions, more selfish; and our afflicting emotions—such as craving and obsession—stronger.

If we notice that we are starting to get attached to the beings for whom we are wishing joy or to the feeling of joy itself, we should meditate on the suffering that beings face and the causes of their suffering, and generate compassion toward them. Meditating on compassion will free us from falling into thoughts of attachment. Longchen Rabjam writes:

> If meditation on loving-kindness is causing
>   attachment, such as getting attached to family,
> Then meditate on compassion—[since thinking
>   about] the causes and effects of suffering will
>   prevent attachment.[192]

Or you could meditate on equanimity to guard against falling into the ditch of attachment. Jigme Lingpa writes:

> If meditation on loving-kindness is causing
>   attachment,
> Move to meditation on equanimity, free from
>   discrimination.[193]

Fourth, teachings on bodhichitta tell us that all suffering is due to grasping at "self"—"me" or "my," "this" or "that"—and viewing it as real. That leads to our desiring attractive things and hating unwanted ones. All peace and happiness, on the other hand, come from wishing joy for others. So, using the tool of mindfulness and awareness, we must guard our mind from drifting into wrong thoughts and desires. Shantideva writes:

> Whatever happiness there is in this world
> Came from wishing happiness for others.
> Whatever suffering there is in this world
> Came from desiring happiness for oneself.
> What more need I say?
> Childish beings exert themselves for their own benefit.
> The Buddha acts for the benefit of others.
> Just look at the difference between them.[194]

Shantideva therefore advises:

> Protect and preserve your mind [from negative
>   thoughts].
> Aside from the discipline of protecting your mind,
> What need is there for many other disciplines? . . .
> Whoever wishes to protect their mind—
> I beg them with folded palms,
> Please maintain mindfulness and awareness,
> Even at the cost of your life![195]

Ngulchu Thogme also stresses the importance of guarding the mind from negativity:

> In brief, whatever activities you do, wherever you are,
> Check the conditions of your mind.
> With mindfulness and awareness,
> Always serve the needs of others.
> This is the practice of bodhisattvas.[196]

17

COMPASSION MEDITATION

YOU MAY HAVE ALREADY LEARNED something about
meditation on "sending and receiving" with compassion,
known as *tonglen* in Tibetan. This chapter offers a meditation that combines sending and receiving with the Four
Buddha Stages.

Begin by enjoying the loving-kindness of the Outer
Buddha with devotion, and let it awaken thoughts and feelings of loving-kindness in your mind as the Inner Buddha.
Then, singing OM MA-NI PAD-ME HUNG, offer to all beings
the radiant blessing lights of wisdom, love, and power of
the Outer and Inner Buddha—that is, of the Buddha of
Loving-Kindness and of yourself.

See and feel that the habitual mental, emotional, and
physical ills of all beings—such as sickness, sadness, pain,
fear, and confusion—take the form of a smoke-like darkness pervading their bodies. The beams, rays, and waves
of light emanating from the Outer Buddha and yourself
completely fill the bodies and minds of all beings with loving-kindness.

The lights dispel all the darkness in every being's
body and mind without leaving a trace. All are filled with
blessing lights of wisdom, love, and power. Every being is

fully transformed into a body of radiant blessing light and a mind of all-knowing wisdom, unconditional love, and boundless power with blessing energy waves resounding to the sounds of OM MA-NI PAD-ME HUNG. Repeat this meditation many times.

After a while, introduce tonglen: offer the radiant blessing lights of loving-kindness to others with the sound of the mantra, as discussed; then joyfully receive their suffering and confusion in the form of smoke-like darkness with the strength to bear anything for them.

Alternatively, as taught in most tonglen practices, offer blessing lights to others with your out-breath to purify them, and lovingly receive their suffering with your in-breath.

Also, once you purify and transform all beings this way, you can receive loving-kindness in the form of waves of light from them with the sound of the sacred mantra. That becomes the blessings from the Universal Buddha.

Finally, think of and feel the oneness of all beings in loving-kindness and rest in that self-awareness without concepts—the Ultimate Buddha.

If you do tonglen with true loving-kindness from the heart, taking in others' ills will not affect you negatively. Your unconditional love will dissolve and transform the negativities you take in. So rather than making you sad, ill, or afraid, this meditation will help you overcome fear, sadness, and negative emotions. It will generate amazing merits of strength, confidence, deep joy, and positive karma. And it will strengthen, refine, and perfect your own experience of loving-kindness.

18

REBIRTH IN THE PURE LAND

ACCORDING TO BUDDHISM, at the time of death, your body will dissolve into the earth forever—but your mind, or consciousness, will survive and take rebirth somewhere. You may be born as a human being or any other kind of being in an infinite world system that is visible or invisible to us. Some will enjoy pleasant and peaceful lives; others will endure suffering and struggle, all depending on the person's past habits and deeds (karma).

What Happens After Death

What happens after death depends on your karma and mental habits. Buddhism teaches that if you have generated wholesome mentalities such as peaceful, joyful, loving thoughts in this life and have served others with such qualities, then because of these positive mental habits and deeds, your mind will have a joyful and beneficial rebirth.

Otherwise, if you have saturated your mind in negative emotions like hatred, jealousy, attachment, and confusion, and have hurt others, then you will take rebirth in a world of endless suffering, fear, sadness, and pain, due to these past negative mental habits and deeds.

Buddhism also teaches that if you have accomplished high stages of meditation, such as the perfection of loving-kindness free from concepts, you could attain Buddhahood during your lifetime or while dying. If you attain Buddhahood, you will no longer have to take rebirth because of your karma or mental habits. Instead, you will be able to manifest multiple emanations (*tulkus*) in various forms to serve others solely out of loving-kindness and compassion.[197]

The Blissful Pure Land

Even if you haven't yet attained Buddhahood, if you have accumulated a great amount of merits, you could take rebirth in a Buddha paradise such as the Blissful Pure Land of the Buddha of Infinite Light (Amitabha) and the Buddha of Loving-Kindness (Avalokiteshvara). The Blissful Pure Land is a peaceful and joyful world of light. After taking rebirth in such a pure land, you will advance uninterruptedly on your spiritual journey to attain Buddhahood within one lifetime.

Shakyamuni Buddha taught his followers to meditate on the following "four causes" of taking rebirth in the Blissful Pure Land. The Buddha said:

O Ananda, there are people who [1] think of the details of the Buddha [of Infinite Light and his Pure Land] again and again. [2] They create many, immeasurable merits. [3] They develop bodhichitta. [4] They dedicate their merits and make aspirations to take rebirth in the Blissful Pure Land. When they die . . . they will take rebirth in the universe of the Blissful Pure Land.[198]

The Four Causes of Rebirth in the Pure Land

1. *Establish the mental habit of being in the Pure Land.* Meditate on seeing all images as the images of the light of loving-kindness of the Buddhas, bodhisattvas, and the Blissful Pure Land. Meditate on hearing all sounds as the sounds of wisdom and unconditional love—OM MA-NI PAD-ME HUNG (or, using the name of Amitabha, OM AMITABHA HRI). Meditate on enjoying all feelings as the experience of unconditional love. This changes the orientation of our mental perception from being in this mundane world to being in the Pure Land.

If our mind has been trained in seeing the Buddha's presence and feeling his qualities while we are alive, then all our experiences in the bardo—the transitional period between death and rebirth—will arise as the boundless visions of the radiant presence of the Buddha of Loving-Kindness and his Pure Land, as well as the feelings of total peace, joy, and loving-kindness. These experiences— wisdom and wisdom-light—are the inherent pure qualities of our mind that we awakened in our mindstream through meditation. Then our experience of rebirth, too, will become the continuation of the joyous experience of the Buddha's qualities.

2. *Accumulate merits to create the positive karma to be reborn in the Pure Land.* One of the most traditional and

comprehensive ways to accumulate merits is to practice the Sevenfold Devotional Practices:

- Paying homage and making offerings
- Purifying negative deeds
- Rejoicing over all virtuous deeds
- Praying for the Buddhas and teachers to live long
- Praying that they give teachings to all
- Dedicating all our merits to all as the cause of their peace, joy, enlightenment, and rebirth in the Pure Land

Especially pray to the Buddha of Loving-Kindness by singing the Six-Syllable Prayer with deep devotion. Then receive the blessing lights of the Buddha's unconditional love, and enjoy and share them with all, over and over again. This generates the main seed of taking rebirth in the Pure Land.

3. *Develop* bodhichitta. Generate the aspiration that every mother-being take rebirth in the Pure Land and attain enlightenment. This fully opens and expands your spiritual potential to take birth in the Pure Land and attain enlightenment. This magnifies the power of your meditation and its effect, as you are working for infinite beings wholeheartedly.

4. *Dedicate the merits.* Dedicate your merits to all beings as the cause of their taking rebirth in the Pure Land for now and for ultimately attaining Buddhahood. Make aspirational prayers for the same. This ensures that the first three causes produce rebirth in the Pure Land.

OR SIMPLY PRAY FOR ALL TO GO TO THE PURE LAND

However, if you simply pray to the Buddha, singing OM MA-NI PAD-ME HUNG with strong devotion and heartfelt loving-kindness for all mother-beings to be born in the Pure Land and attain Buddhahood—that will cover all four causes.

Even if your meditation is not pure or strong enough to take rebirth in the Pure Land, praying with devotion to the Buddha of Loving-Kindness for all beings to be reborn in the Pure Land, will still help you secure a more peaceful and joyful death, journey through the bardo, and have a happier rebirth in a healthier world.

Also, if someone else is dying or dead, with thoughts of loving-kindness toward them and all beings, pray to the Buddha and his Pure Land with devotion and sing OM MA-NI PAD-ME HUNG. Think and feel that the dying or deceased person is also joining you in prayer with devotion from the heart. Visualize that the dying or dead person is receiving blessing lights, lights of loving-kindness from the Buddha. All the negative effects of their unhealthy karma, in the form of darkness, are fully purified. They fully transform into a wholesome person of blessing light of loving-kindness and take instant rebirth (called a "lotus birth") in the Pure Land.[199]

So in meditation and daily life, think and feel repeatedly that you are in the Pure Land of the Buddha of Loving-Kindness. See every mother-being as enjoying the Pure Land. Make aspirations for them to be reborn there. Try to remember to pray and enjoy the Buddha's presence and blessings at the time of death, and especially try to remember him after death. Then you will die peacefully and joyfully, as you will be going to your joyful home, the Pure Land, from which you will be able to serve others. When you leave, a world of peace and joy, the Pure Land, will arise before you for you to take instant rebirth in.[200]

PART FOUR

THE PRACTICES
IN BRIEF

19

Prayer Texts

THE FOLLOWING short esoteric meditation distills the essence of the practices we have been discussing. It is an important recitation liturgy and meditation formula on the Buddha of Loving-Kindness that was mystically revealed as a *ter* by Rigdzin Godem (1337–1408).

This chapter has three sections. The first section, "Preliminary Practices," corresponding to the First Buddha Stage, includes going for refuge, developing bodhichitta, and a devotional prayer. The second section, "Main Meditation," corresponds to the Second, Third, and Fourth Buddha Stages. The concluding section is "Dedication and Aspiration Prayers." If you can, practice all three sections of this chapter in one sitting. However, if you don't have enough time or are not ready, then you could practice the Preliminary Practices and the Dedication and Aspiration Prayers, focusing mainly on the devotional practices that center on the Six-Syllable Prayer.

Preliminary Practices

GOING FOR REFUGE IN THE THREE JEWELS

We start by going for refuge in the Three Jewels. We take refuge in the Buddha as the guide who leads us to the goal,

Buddhahood. We take refuge in the Dharma as the path, including practices like devotion, loving-kindness, and the Six Perfections, in order to reach the goal. We take refuge in the realized Sangha, the religious community of fellow practitioners, as the support for our journey along the path of Dharma to reach the attainment of enlightenment.

Take refuge in the Three Jewels by reciting the following lines with devotion from the depth of your heart with total trust:

> To the excellent Buddha, Dharma, and Sangha,
> I go for refuge until the attainment of enlightenment.
> By the merits of generosity and other virtues,
> May we attain Buddhahood for the benefit of all the
>   beings.
> *[Repeat three times.]*

Note that in the third line above, the word "others" refers to the rest of the Six Perfections—that is, the merits of generosity, discipline, patience, diligence, contemplation, and wisdom.

DEVELOPING BODHICHITTA

You are now ready to develop bodhichitta through the four boundless attitudes—loving-kindness, compassion, sympathetic joy, and equanimity—toward all.

> May all beings enjoy happiness and the causes of
>   happiness.

May all beings be free from suffering and the causes
of suffering.
May all beings never be dissociated from the supreme
happiness, free from suffering.
May all beings remain in boundless equanimity, free
from both attachment to kin and hatred of foes.
[Repeat three times.]

PRAYER TO THE BUDDHA OF LOVING-KINDNESS

Visualize the Buddha of Loving-Kindness in the sky before
you. Think about and feel his unconditional love. Bathe in
his loving presence. Fully focusing your mind with devotion and trust in him from the depth of your heart, recite
these five lines:

O Blessed One, Buddha of Great Loving-Kindness,
Your complexion is white, as you are unstained by any
defect.
Your crown is adorned by the Fully Enlightened One
[Amitabha Buddha].
Your eyes of loving-kindness watch over all beings.
O Buddha of Loving-Kindness—to you I pray.[201]

If you are going to focus on the main meditation, you
can do so now without repeating the Six-Syllable Prayer
here. Otherwise, sing the Six-Syllable Prayer over and over
again, until the experience of the Buddha's loving-kindness registers deep in your being:

OM MA-NI PAD-ME HUNG

If you can generate true loving-kindness in your heart through devotional prayer to the Buddha of Loving-Kindness, as the Outer Buddha meditation, you will make enormous merits, accomplish spiritual attainments, and be able to serve others greatly.

The Main Meditation

The main meditation embodies what is known in esoteric Buddhism as the development stage and the perfection stage. In essence, they are the trainings in the last three Buddha Stages—the Inner, Universal, and Ultimate Buddhas.

This meditation is the heart essence of the teachings of Sutra and Tantra. It is highly blessed, as it was taught and concealed by Guru Padmasambhava and discovered by Rigdzin Godem as a *ter*, or mystical revelation. It is warm with the blessed breaths of many Masters, as it has been practiced and transmitted to us through an uninterrupted chain of great adepts.

THE WISH-FULFILLING GEM: THE LITURGY OF THE BUDDHA OF LOVING-KINDNESS

The following is the translation of a brief *sadhana,* or esoteric liturgy, titled *Thugje Chenpo'i Ngöntok Yidzin Norbu.*[202]

Homage to Avalokiteshvara!

HRI! Through the meditation of instant recollection, I visualize myself [as follows]:

In the emptiness state, on a lotus and moon seat, arises

A white lotus adorned with a HRI syllable, which then transforms

Into the Lord of Loving-Kindness, Noble Avalokiteshvara.

His body is radiantly white with one face and four arms.

The palms of his first two hands are joined at his heart.

His second right hand holds a mala of precious crystal.

His second left hand holds a white lotus by the stem.

His face is smiling; his eyes are clear and his nose is high.

His dark bluish hair is swirled up in a bun [at the top of his head].

Above the crown of his head sits the Buddha of Infinite Light, as his Crown Lord.

At the heart of my visualized self

I imagine a blossoming white lotus with six petals. At its center

Is a HRI syllable. On the six petals are the Six Syllables:

OM MA-NI PAD-ME HUNG.

Lights are projected from my body [as the Buddha].

All forms become divine forms, the union of emptiness and appearances—

The Great Loving-Kindness One, the King of the Noble Ones.

Lights project from the mantra [syllables at my heart], and all sounds such as the sounds of the elements

Become the sounds of mantra, the union of emptiness
and sound.
Recollections and thoughts remain in the state of
freedom from arising, abiding, and cessation.
Rest in the realization that transcends all thoughts,
expressions, and designations.
By visualizing thus, I recite the Six Syllables, the
esoteric mantra,
Hundreds, thousands, tens of thousands, and
hundreds of thousands of times—clearly.
OM MA-NI PAD-ME HUNG.

Occasionally, offer offerings, praise, and supplications. Dedicate virtuous deeds to the cause of enlightenment. *The Wish-Fulfilling Gem: The Liturgy of the Buddha of Loving-Kindness* is completed. Samaya. RGYA RGYA RGYA. This text was discovered by Tulku Rigdzin Chenmo[203] as a *ter* from the Western Copper Red Treasure Box. Thus, seeing oneself as indivisible from the body, speech, and mind of the Buddha of Loving-Kindness and contemplating in that state, recite the mantra of the Buddha of Loving-Kindness—OM MA-NI PAD-ME HUNG—hundreds, thousands, tens of thousands, hundreds of thousands, millions, tens of millions, a hundred million times and more.

Dedication and Aspiration Prayers

Between the recitations and meditations, and especially at the end of each meditation session, dedicate the merits accumulated through your prayers, meditations, and virtuous deeds to all mother-beings with great joy, as the cause of their having peace and happiness for now, and ultimately attaining enlightenment. With the dedicated merits as the seed, make heartfelt aspirations for all mother-beings by reciting the following prayers found in the *Avatamsaka Sutra,*[204] the *Bodhicharyavatara,*[205] and other sacred texts:

Just as the conqueror Manjushri realized [the truth]
And as Samantabhadra[206] did—
For the purpose of following them,
I fully dedicate all these virtuous deeds.

The precious bodhichitta,
If it has not yet arisen, may it arise [in all].
If it has arisen, may it never decay.
May it increase further and further.

As long as space remains,
As long as mother-beings remain,
May I remain [in this world] and
Pacify the suffering of mother-beings.

Those beings who are ill,
May they swiftly be healed from their sicknesses.
May all beings' sicknesses, without remainder,
Never occur again.

From here, in the direction of the West,
There is the Pure Land of the Buddha of Infinite
    Light.
Whoever says his name in prayer,
May they [all] be born in his supreme Pure Land.

By the power of these merits, may we swiftly
Become one with the Buddha of Loving-Kindness.
May all beings without exception
Attain the state of [the Buddha of Loving-Kindness].

By the blessings of the Buddha, who has attained the
    three bodies;
By the power of the truth of the changeless state, the
    ultimate Dharma nature;
By the power of the truth of the Sangha, which never
    deviates from realization—
May the dedications and the aspirations that we have
    made be realized, as we have made them.

20

THE FOUR-STAGE
MEDITATIONS IN BRIEF

MANY PEOPLE COMPLAIN that they cannot do Dharma practice because they don't have the time or energy. Although meditating for longer periods is better, you can still profit from shorter sessions that will fit into your daily schedule. Meditating for only 30 minutes will be highly beneficial, especially if you can do it every day and with heartfelt concentration and devotion. The following is a sample of how you can do the Four Stages of Buddha meditation in just 30 minutes or even less.

If you are beginning, spend 10 minutes for the First Stage, 10 minutes for the Second, 3 minutes for the Third Stage, and 2 minutes for the Fourth Stage. Each Stage will flow naturally into the next, if you do the preceding stages properly. Take 3 minutes to settle down the mind at the beginning and 2 more minutes to conclude the meditation at the end. Once you've done the meditation daily for a month or so and have made some progress, you can readjust the length of time for each stage, as you wish.

Sit in a comfortable place that is suitable for you. Take a few deep breaths in order to release any worries or stress. Feel good and thankful for the opportunity to have the time to do meditation.

Setting Your Intention for the Meditation

Start the meditation by developing the attitude of enlightenment. Think and say to yourself: *I am making a vow to bring happiness with its causes and enlightenment to all mother-beings.* By launching yourself into the meditation with this intention, you greatly expand the scope of your mental resolution and power.

First Stage: Meditation on the Outer Buddha

You are now ready to start with the Outer Buddha. Visualize, feel, and believe that the Buddha of Loving-Kindness is in front of you, looking at you and thinking of you with all-knowing wisdom, boundless power, and especially loving-kindness, unconditional love. Feel the intimacy with the Buddha.

Pray with devotion: Then pray by chanting OM MA-NI PAD-ME HUNG with heartfelt devotion that opens your heart with the energy of joy of being in the presemce of the Buddha of Loving-Kindness. Trust in his presence, his love, and his enlightened qualities.

Receive blessing: Then, from the Buddha's body, visualize and feel that his blessings come in the form of infinite beams of rainbow light, lights of his wisdom, love, and power with energy waves of blissful heat. These bright lights of loving-kindness—wishing joy for all—enter your body, and all your unwholesome thoughts, negative emotions, and evil deeds (karma), as well as your suffering, are totally dispelled in the form of darkness from every particle of your body. Do this over and over again.

Transformation: Every particle of your body is purified and filled with—and then transformed into—the blessing lights of wisdom, power, and especially loving-kindness of the Buddha. See every breath as the blessing waves of blissful heat of love with the sounds of OM MA-NI PAD-ME HUNG. You must recognize the transformation that is taking place in you and enjoy it again and again.

Second Stage: Meditation on the Inner Buddha

You are now ready for the Inner Buddha. Since your mind changes according to what and how you see, think, feel, and believe, you should now see and recognize that through the power of meditating on the Buddha and his loving-kindness, your mind has become a mind of loving-kindness. Loving-kindness, embodying the pure qualities of your mind, has now awakened. See, feel, and rejoice and celebrate over that great transformation.

Serve others with loving-kindness: Then, with that newfound heart of loving-kindness, inwardly look at your loving mother (or any beloved individual) with strong feelings of unconditional love from the depth of your heart. See that lights of love, wisdom, and power, with waves of blissful heat energy and the sound of mantra, come to her from the Buddha who is before you as well as from your own transformed blessing light body. These lights of unconditional love dispel the darkness and suffering from her body. Her body and mind transform into a body and mind of the light of wisdom, love, and power with the energy waves and the sounds of mantra. Her body becomes a body of blessing light, a mind of wisdom, power, unconditional love, joy, and peace. Chant OM MA-NI PAD-ME HUNG many times.

Then, with a heart of loving-kindness, gradually share the blessings of the Buddha and yourself with other friends in the same way. Extend the blessings to strangers, then foes, and finally infinite mother-beings. All have become a universe of light and love, peace and joy, with waves of OM MA-NI PAD-ME HUNG.

Third Stage: Meditation on the Universal Buddha

Move now to the Universal Buddha Stage. The qualities of your mental objects, the world, become what your mind sees, thinks, and feels. So see that all forms that your mind is seeing are images of light with the qualities of loving-kindness. Hear that all sounds that your mind is hearing are sounds with the qualities of loving-kindness—OM MA-NI PAD-ME HUNG. Feel that all experiences you are having are feelings of loving-kindness—unconditional and boundless love. Enjoying loving-kindness with this awakened openness and universal dimension, we meditate and pray.

Fourth Stage: Meditation on the Ultimate Buddha

Finally, rest in the Ultimate Buddha, the state of awareness of unconditioned openness and boundless loving-kindness—without grasping or conceptualizing at all. Even your senses are suspended. That doesn't mean that you can't hear or see; just that you are seeing and hearing through the power of awareness wisdom, with total openness and oneness without duality followed by emotions, sensations, and so on. Keep going back to that openness nature of loving-kindness and resting in it again and again. Then, slowly, the loving-kindness that you are experiencing could become a state that is free from concepts, the union of loving-kindness and emptiness—the true nature of the mind.

Concluding Meditations

Conclude the meditation with Dedication and Aspirations. Dedicate the merits that you accumulated by offering them to all mother-beings as the cause of their happiness and enlightenment. Then make aspirations that, as the result, every mother-being may enjoy happiness, peace, and joy, and attain Buddhahood.

Closing Verse

The sun of this life is fast setting behind the tall
  mountains in the West.
But, if the light of unconditional love is secure in our
  heart core,
Forever will it remain as the source of the timeless
  light of wisdom and love.
I have tried to share this message with all who care to
  lend an ear.

Though my own mindstream is ruled by the wildest
  emotions,
What I have offered here is the pristine ambrosia
  cherished by the Awakened Sages,
Unstained by the reckless blurting of my own
  mundane jabber.
So it is worth your picking it up with respect and
  enshrining it in your heart.

By the power of the refuges—the Three Precious
  Jewels,
The Masters of Accomplishments, the Seekers of
  Enlightenment and the Angels of Wisdom—

May all mindstreams that are touched by these
  messages of love
Be united with the true loving-kindness, bodhichitta.

NOTES

Titles of Tibetan texts are abbreviated in the notes; see the Bibliography for the complete data. The word "folio" in the notes refers to the Tibetan style of pagination, and "p." (for "page") is used for the Western style of pagination. When paginations from traditional Tibetan sources are cited, the abbreviated title is followed by the folio number. Where relevant, the front and back of the folio is indicated by letter *a* or *b*, respectively; and then the line number follows the slash mark (for example: "CT, folio 244a/1").

Opening Verse

1. Tib. drupchen, *grub chen*; Skt. *mahasiddha*. Here this refers to Kyabje Dodrupchen Rinpoche the Fourth, who is my root teacher. Here, *Do* (*rdo*) is "stone," and *Drupchen* means the "great adept": "the Great Adept from the Stone Valley." The main Monastery of the Dodrupchen lineage in Eastern Tibet is also known as the Dodrupchen Monastery, where I studied.

2. Tib. rigdzin, *rig 'dzin*; Skt. *vidyadhara*. The realized Masters of esoteric (tantric) teachings of Buddhism.

3. Bodhisattvas are the trainees and the highly realized Masters of exoteric (Sutra) teachings of Buddhism.

4. Tib. khandro, *mkha' 'gro*; Skt. *dakini*. Highly realized female teachers of esoteric (tantric) teachings of Buddhism.

5. Ngodrub Palbar Ling (dngos sgrub dpal 'bar gling), or

Blazing Glorious Seat of Accomplishments, is a name for
Dodrupchen Monastery, where I grew up as a novice and
as a young tulku in training.

Chapter 1: The Importance of Training Our Mind

6. LS, folio 246b/4.
7. The Third Dodrupchen was Jigme Tenpe Nyima (1865–1926).
   Dodrupchen means "*mahasiddha* [great adept] of the Do Valley."
8. KDL, p. 202/16.
9. Maitreya-natha is a bodhisattva who is said to be currently residing in Tushita Heaven, ready to descend to the
   Jambu continent (our world) as our next Buddha. Asanga
   had a vision of Maitreya-natha, who revealed many teachings to him. Asanga wrote them down, and they became the
   famous Five Texts of Maitreya, upon which the Yogachara,
   or Mind-Only, school of philosophy was founded. Many,
   however, credit Asanga as the actual author of the texts and
   founder of the Yogachara school.
10. GB, p. 6/3.
11. CT, folio 244a/1.
12. DDN, folio 25a/3.
13. GR, folio 200a/4.
14. TBN, folio 123b/4.
15. DNC, folio 172a/1.
16. BGD, folio 16b/2.
17. GR, folio 187b/5.
18. Konchog Dronme (1859–1936) was an esteemed scholar and
    adept of Dodrupchen Monastery.
19. TBS, p. 10/3.

Chapter 2: Essential Tools for Meditation

20. Padmasambhava (Skt. "Lotus-Born"; Tib. Pema Jungne,
    padma 'byung gnas). One of the greatest adepts and teach-

ers of esoteric Buddhism, known popularly in Tibet as Guru Rinpoche ("Precious Teacher"). He traveled from India to Tibet in the eighth century and founded Tibetan Buddhism, tamed human and nonhuman forces opposing the Dharma, transmitted Vajrayana (esoteric) teachings, and through his mystical power concealed teachings and religious objects for future followers to find. Those concealed teachings and treasures (*terma*) are still being discovered in Tibet. See *Masters of Meditation and Miracles* by Tulku Thondup.

21. SLD, discovered by Rigdzin Godem as a *ter* text, folio 44a/4.

22. GB, p. 3/16.

23. This is a summary of a sutra quoted in GP, folio 475b/1.

24. DDRS, p. 96/11.

25. See Glossary for pronunciation.

26. See *Avalokiteshvara* in the Glossary for pronunciation.

27. Shantideva (eighth century) was an Indian scholar who wrote the well-known *Bodhicharyavatara*, a guide to the bodhisattva's way of life.

28. BP, folio 95a/4.

29. TY, p. 241/16.

30. Patrul Rinpoche (1808–1887) was a great Master with a nonsectarian approach. Among his major works that are well known in English translation are *Treasury of Precious Qualities* and *The Words of My Perfect Teacher*.

31. The four actions are pacifying, increasing, overpowering, and demolishing. See Tulku Thondup, *The Healing Power of Loving Kindness*, pp. 79–91.

32. TTB, pp. 351–364.

33. BN, p. 58/12.

34. KBZ, p. 439/15.

35. Kyala Khenpo Chechog Dondrub Tsal (1893–1957) of Dodrupchen Monastery was Tulku Thondup's tutor.

36. RZD, folio 26a/2.

37. Karma Lingpa (1326–1386) was a revealer of *ter*, notably the famous text popularly known as the Tibetan Book of the Dead.
38. ZTR, folio 7a/1.
39. STG, folio 5b/3.
40. Shantarakshita (eighth-ninth century) was an Indian Master who was abbot of Nalanda University. He ordained the first Tibetans and established the first monastic community in Tibet (Samye Monastery).
41. DGT, folio 700/6.
42. KZBZ, p. 317/14.
43. Tib. *ye shes kyi rang od; ye shes kyi od; ye shes kyi gdangs;* and *rig gdangs*.
44. KD, folio 3a/3.

Chapter 3: Devotion and Trust

45. BP, folio 72/4.
46. Tib. depa, *dad pa,* popularly translated as "faith."
47. Four trusts: dangwa (*dang ba,* joyous clarity), döpa ('*dod pa,* yearning trust), yiche (*yid ch'es,* confident trust), and chirmi dokpa (*phyir mi ldog pa,* irreversible trust).
48. Jigme Lingpa (1730–1798) was the discoverer of the Longchen Nyingthig teachings as a *ter*.
49. YD, p. 33/15.
50. BP, folio 71a/2.
51. SLD, folio 44a/4.
52. See BLC (*Lamrim Ch'eba*), p. 138/9.
53. YD, p. 34/3.
54. D. T. Suzuki, *Buddha of Infinite Light,* p. 26.
55. Tagtu Ngu (Tib. rtag tu ngu; Skt. Sadaparudita, the "Ever-Weeping Bodhisattva") was a disciple mentioned in the Prajnaparamita scriptures as a perfect example of devotion and perseverance.
56. GT, folio 276b/4.

57. Kunkhyen [Omniscient] Longchen Rabjam (1308–1363) was the greatest Dzogchen master of the Nyingma school of Tibetan Buddhism.
58. YRD, folio 31a/4.
59. KT, folio 63b/6. The Buddha's figurative offspring are the bodhisattvas.
60. CT, folio 245a/1.
61. DTG, folio 97b/5.
62. KT, folio 63b/5.
63. GB, p. 19/19.
64. GB, p. 36/5.
65. Blofeld, *Bodhisattva of Compassion*, pp. 110–115.
66. CCL, folio 166a/3.

Chapter 4: The Essence of Loving-Kindness

67. LS, folio 246b/4.
68. CT, folio 245a/1.
69. TY, p. 209/15. The Tibetan wording here is *snying rje stong nyid kyi snying po chan zhes dmigs med kyi snying rje.*
70. BP, folio 4b/4.
71. BP, folio 5a/2.
72. DTG, p. 491/9.
73. PHC, folio 361a/6.
74. Pandita Padma Wangchen (1870–?) was a great scholar, monk, and tertön, one of the few tertöns who was also a monk.
75. DNN, folio 10b/1.
76. BM, folio 130b/2.
77. See *four virtuous attitudes* in the Glossary.
78. See *four boundless attitudes* in the Glossary.
79. KBZ, p. 347/6.
80. SN, folio 27b/2.
81. *snying po mch'og gi mdo,* quoted in YNG, folio 43b/2.

82. TZG, folio 19a/6.

83. Tib. *bsam pa bzang po,* "good thoughts." See KBZ, p. 347/9.

84. These are well-known lines recited by all the different schools of Tibetan Buddhism. However, I don't know who composed them.

85. NTG, p. 3/11.

86. DDRS, p. 440/2.

87. Tib. chökyi rangzhin, *ch'os kyi rang bzhin,* "nature of phenomena."

88. Tib. *don dam sems bskyed.* See TR, p. 138/10.

89. "Free from elaborations," Tib. *spros bral.*

90. The First Dodrupchen, Jigme Thrinle Ozer (1745–1821), was the first of the Dodrupchen incarnation lineage. *Dodrupchen* means "*mahasiddha* [great adept] of the Do Valley."

91. Victorious One(s): an epithet for the Buddha or those who are like the Buddha.

92. GCT, p. 293/21.

93. BG, folio 132a/3.

94. TY, p. 195/7.

95. Nagarjuna (ca. 150–250) was one of the most celebrated philosophers of the Buddhist world and the founder of the Madhyamaka, the Middle Way school of Mahayana Buddhism.

96. RP, p. 122/6.

97. TG, p. 111b/3.

98. BM, folio 132a/3.

99. TG, p. 106/4.

100. Tib. *rdo rje rtse mo.* SDT, folios 142b/1–274a/5.

101. TGR, folio 39a/4.

102. SN, folio 28b/2.

103. "Contaminated happiness" is happiness contaminated by concepts and emotions; it is not ultimate happiness, which is freedom from dualistic and conceptual sensations.

104. BLC, p. 304/19.

Chapter 5: The Four Buddha Stages

105. DP, folio 168ba/1.
106. BP, folio 38a/2.
107. In Buddhist teachings, Avalokiteshvara is portrayed both as a Buddha and as Buddha's manifestation as a bodhisattva.
108. CYD, folio 84a/5.
109. Rigdzin Godem (1337–1408) was one of the greatest tertöns (Tib. *gter ston*), or discoverers of mystical teachings (*ter*).
110. YN, folios 211–214.
111. KSG, folio 9b/3.
112. DMZ, folio 201b/1.

Chapter 6: Meditation on the Outer Buddha

113. The Buddha does not have flesh skin. He is made of light, and even that is wisdom-light. Nonetheless, it is taught that his complexion is white. The color has significance for our meditation. Whatever colors we are visualizing, we must understand them in their best symbolic qualities, such as white representing purity as well as calmness and peacefulness.
114. Tib. 32 tsen zangpo (*mtshan bzang po*) and 80 peje (*dpe byad*).
115. Five silken garments and eight jewel ornaments: The five silk garments are the head scarf, upper garment, lower garment, belt, and shawl. The eight jewel ornaments are the crown, earrings, short necklace, armlets, long necklace, bracelets, finger rings, and anklets. See KBZ, p. 436/14.
116. TY, p. 237/19.
117. See John Blofeld, *Bodhisattva of Compassion*.
118. TTB, p. 361/5.
119. GP, folio 497a/2.
120. SMC, p. 477/16.
121. If you are saying or chanting the Six Syllables according to

common Buddhist practice, it is a prayer. If you are chanting it as an esoteric training, it is a mantra. But here we are calling it a prayer.

122. TY, p. 250/19.

123. TY, p. 251/2.

124. Tib. *snying rje stong nyid kyi snying po chan.*

125. Emotional obscurations and intellectual obscurations.

126. TY, pp. 123–271.

127. TY, p. 250/19.

128. Karma Chagme, Raga Asya (1613–1678), was a lineage holder of the Karma Kagyu tradition of Tibetan Buddhism.

Chapter 7: Meditation on the Inner Buddha

129. RCZ, folio 68b/6.

130. *dharani* (Skt.): A long mantra; a sacred Sanskrit phrase or the essence of a text.

131. TBT, folio 3b/1. Dege Edition. "Nonreturners" (Skt. *anagamin*) refers to the stage of one of the high attainments of the Buddhist path of training.

132. ZGD, p. 81/6.

133. Skt. *sugata;* Tib. dewar shekpa; *bde bar gshegs pa,* one who has "gone to bliss."

Chapter 8: Meditation on the Universal Buddha

134. PHC, folio 359a/1.

135. PT, folio 261a/4.

136. DTG, folio 68b/7.

137. KT, folio 201a/2.

138. OKD, folio 251a/7.

139. ST, folio 92b/3.

Chapter 9: Meditation on the Ultimate Buddha

140. See *five wisdoms of Buddhahood* in the Glossary.

141. SNR, folio 191b/2. "Water-tree" is the name of a tree given in

ancient Indian Buddhist texts. It is related to the plantain tree. It holds a tremendous amount of water in its trunk, and is thought to be very fragile and unstable. It gives fruits once and then perishes. So here, it symbolizes something unsubstantial.

142. RP, p. 78/5.

143. BP, folio 80a/1.

144. Ngulchu Thogme (1295–1369), a Master of the Kadam school, was the author of the classic *Thirty-seven Verses on the Practice of a Bodhisattva*.

145. GLL, p. 7/8.

146. *Drachen Dzinkyi Yumla Todpa* (Praise to the Mother by Rahula). Je Gampopa quotes this in TG (Jewel Ornament of Liberation), p. 289/17.

147. GB, p. 19/21.

148. Manjushrimitra was an Indian Master of the Dzogpa Chenpo lineage and a chief disciple of Prahevajra (Garab Dorje).

149. Prahevajra, an Indian teacher known in Tibetan as Garab Dorje, was the first human Master of the Dzogpa Chenpo teachings of the Nyingma lineage of Tibetan Buddhism.

150. Quoted in KBZ, p. 554/7.

151. No-self (Skt. *anatman*; Tib. dagme, *bdag med*) is the absence of a permanent, fixed, independent "self" in phenomena—a central teaching of Buddhism.

152. ZLB, folio 523a/3.

Chapter 10: Enhance the Effects

153. Asanga was the fourth-century founder of the Yogachara school and the author of many important treatises. Asanga had a vision of Maitreya-natha, who revealed many teachings to him. See also note 9.

154. NKT, folio 5b/3.

155. BP, folio 32a/2.

Chapter 11: Move Forward Step by Step

156. BLC, p. 306/18.
157. RP, p. 96/12.
158. For more on the intermediate stage, or bardo, see *Peaceful Death, Joyful Rebirth* by Tulku Thondup.
159. BTT, p. 35/4.
160. See YRD, folio 44b/2; DTS, p. 371/5; and GSG, p. 55b/7.
161. SR, folio 4a/6.
162. Kamalashila (Tib. Peme Ngang Tsul; ca. 740–795) was the main disciple of Shantarakshita.
163. GRT, folio 61b/3.
164. GRT, folio 62b/6.
165. CRN, p. 162/1.

Chapter 13: The Benefits of Loving-Kindness Meditation

166. TG, quoted in BLC, p. 305/1.
167. JZK, folio 262b/6.
168. BM, folio 131a/2.
169. SNR, folio 192b/5.
170. SNR, folio 198b/4.
171. BLC, p. 305/16.
172. BGD, folio 270a/4.
173. RP, p. 102/2.
174. BLC, p. 305/16.
175. RP, p. 95/3. See also the Glossary entry *three bodies*.
176. RCZ, folio 37b/3.

Chapter 14: Healing Physical and Mental Ills

177. DP, folio 168b/1.
178. BP, folio 68a/5.
179. Buddha's common teachings are preserved in three collections or divisions. In Sanskrit they are known as Tripitaka (lit. "three baskets") and in Tibetan Denösum (*sde*

snod gsum). They are Vinaya, which is the collections of Buddha's teachings on discipline; Sutra, the discourses on meditation; and Abhidharma, the teachings on wisdom and metaphysics.

180. Jowo or Jowoje Atisha (980–1054) was one of the greatest Buddhist Masters, who propagated Buddhism in Asia. He was born in Bengal, India, and died in Tibet.

181. TY, p. 172/1.

182. KDL. For an English translation, see Tulku Thondup, *Enlightened Living*, pp. 117–129.

183. ZPD, p. 443/2.

184. KDL, p. 196/6.

Chapter 15: Dealing with Challenging People

185. KBZ, p. 202/17.

186. KBZ, p. 200/10. For the seven unvirtuous deeds of body and speech, see chapter 11.

187. BP, folio 38b/1.

Chapter 16: Daily Activities as Training in Loving-Kindness

188. KBZ, p. 415/2.

189. GLL, p. 4/6.

190. KBZ, p. 384/14.

191. KBZ, p. 318/19.

192. SN, folio 29b/1.

193. YD, p. 40/2.

194. BP, folio 96b/5.

195. BP, folio 34a/3.

196. GLL, p. 9/16.

Chapter 18: Rebirth in the Pure Land

197. See Tulku Thondup, *Peaceful Death, Joyful Rebirth*, chap. 7.

198. OKD, folio 258a/7.

199. For more information, read *Peaceful Death, Joyful Rebirth* and *The Healing Power of Loving-Kindness,* both by Tulku Thondup.

200. For details, please see Tulku Thondup, *Peaceful Death, Joyful Rebirth.*

Chapter 19: Prayer Texts

201. These five lines are a well-known prayer, but I am not sure of the source.

202. TYN, folios 211–212.

203. This is one of the alternate names of Rigdzin Godem (1337–1408).

204. PHC, folio 361b/5.

205. BP.

206. Here, "Samantabhadra" refers to the bodhisattva and disciple of the Buddha.

GLOSSARY

The following language abbreviations are used below: Tib. = Tibetan; Skt. = Sanskrit. The primary languages of the Tibetan canon are Sanskrit and Tibetan. In this Glossary, Sanskrit is spelled in a simplified phonetic manner. If the Sanskrit term is the more frequently used one, it is placed first. Where two terms are given in Tibetan, the first (in Roman type) is the phonetic spelling indicating pronunciation; the second (in italics), is the transliteration. For example, the Tibetan word for loving-kindness is pronounced *jampa*, while the transliteration of the word is *byams pa*.

Abhidharma. Collection of the Buddha's teachings on wisdom and metaphysics, part of the Tripitaka. *See* common teachings.

absolute truth. *See* two truths.

afflicting emotions (Skt. *klesha;* Tib. nyön mong, *nyon mong* or *nyon mong pa*). Unwholesome, destructive, or negative emotions, such as anger and jealousy, which lead to negative actions and thus to suffering. Many translations are possible for this term, including mental or emotional afflictions, defilements, and poisons.

all-evenness (Tib. *mnyam nyid;* Skt. *samata*). Also called ever-evenness or evenness state. State of sameness, equality; all things equally having the nature of emptiness.

Amitabha Buddha. The Buddha of Infinite Light (Skt. Amitabha; Tib. Opagme, *'od dpag med*). The Buddha who presides over the Blissful Pure Land. The name Amitabha has been translated as "Infinite Light" or "Boundless Light." Eons ago, Amitabha was a monk who vowed to liberate beings who invoke his name with devotion. When he attained Buddhahood, his vows resulted in the universe of the Blissful Pure Land. Thus, by the power of his vow or aspiration, the Blissful Pure Land is manifested for the sake of beings, for them to take rebirth there. *See also* Blissful Pure Land.

aspirational bodhichitta (Tib. mönpa semkye, *smon pa sems bskyed*). The first stage of developing bodhichitta, in which the meditator trains in wishing happiness and enlightenment for all. *See also* engaged bodhichitta.

aspirations (Tib. *smon sems*). Wishing others well and praying accordingly.

Avalokiteshvara (Skt., pronounced either *ah-va-lo-ki-TAY-shva-rah* or *ah-va-lo-ki-tay-SHVA-rah*). *See* Buddha of Loving-Kindness.

awareness wisdom (Tib. rigpa'i yeshe; *rig pa'i ye shes*). The true nature of the mind, essentially the same as emptiness and openness wisdom, except that it emphasizes the awareness aspect of wisdom.

bardo (Tib. *bar do*). The transitional period through which we all go between our physical death and rebirth.

beings, sentient. Living beings, both visible and from unseen realms.

blessing lights. Lights of loving-kindness from the Buddha. In meditation we see the Buddha's blessings in the form of light, but this is not ordinary light, like sunlight or flickering star light, but is the self-radiation of the enlightened nature itself. Visualizing the pure light or receiving blessings in the form of light is a process of bringing blessing energies into our minds so that we can purify and transform our mental view and feeling into the realization of Buddha-wisdom.

blissful heat (Tib. dedrö, *bde drod*). The healing, blessing energy of light, visualized as joyful beams of love and power that purify and heal; the caressing, nurturing warmth of loving-kindness energy.

Blissful Pure Land (Skt. Sukhavati; Tib. Dewachen, *bde ba chan*). The Pure Land of the Buddha of Infinite Light (Amitabha), and also the Pure Land of Avalokiteshvara. If we are not certain about attaining Buddhahood at the time of death, we must pray and meditate to take rebirth in the Blissful Pure Land in order to have a peaceful and joyful rebirth where we will be able to attain Buddhahood before long. *See also* Amitabha Buddha; pure land.

bodhichitta (Tib. jangsem, *byang sems*). The aspiration or vow to bring happiness and Buddhahood to all beings and to put that aspiration or vow into practice by training in loving-kindness, devotion, the Six Perfections, and so on. This is the main path of Mahayana followers. *Bodhichitta* has been translated as enlightened mind, enlightened attitude, awakened mind, and awakened heart. Here, however, we are using the Sanskrit word.

There are two aspects to bodhichitta: relative bodhichitta (Tib. kündzop jangsem, *kun rdzob byang sems*) and absolute bodhichitta (Tib. döndam jangsem, *don dam byang sems*). In developing relative bodhichitta, there are two stages: *see* aspirational bodhichitta; engaged bodhichitta.

bodhisattva (Skt.; Tib. jangchup sempa, *byang ch'ub sems dpa'*). Bodhisattvas are trainees and highly realized Masters of exoteric teachings of Buddhism. A bodhisattva's unconditional love for all beings manifests in acts of compassion, charity, and selflessness.

Buddha of Infinite Life (Tib. Tsepakme, *tshe dpag med*; Skt. Amitayus). An aspect of Amitabha, the Buddha of Infinite Light. Amitabha appears in Nirmanakaya form and leads devotees to his Blissful Pure Land at their death. As Amitayus, he manifests in Sambhogakaya form and bestows longevity on his devotees. They are the same Buddha, but with different names owing to different qualities and actions.

Buddha of Infinite Light. *See* Amitabha Buddha.

Buddha of Loving-Kindness (Skt., Avalokiteshvara; Tib. Chenrezi, *spyan ras gzigs*). Avalokiteshvara, who is popularly known in English as the Buddha of Compassion. However, in this book he is called the Buddha of Loving-Kindness, since he is a Buddha of both loving-kindness and compassion, and the meditation discussed here focuses on loving-kindness.

Buddhahood. Enlightenment. The attainment of the three bodies and five wisdoms of Buddhahood.

Buddha-nature. The true nature of the mind; the awakened state (Buddhahood).

celestial realms (Skt. *brahmaloka*). Heavenly planes of existence where beings of the form or formless spheres dwell.

common teachings. The Buddhist tradition based on the sutras, the words of the historical Buddha, Shakyamuni. Buddha's common teachings are preserved in three collections or divisions (Skt. Tripitaka, "three baskets"; Tib. denösum, *sde snod gsum*): Vinaya, the collection of teachings on discipline; Sutra, the discourses on meditation; and Abhidharma, the teachings on wisdom and metaphysics. *See also* Sutra.

compassion (Tib. nyingje, *snying rje*; Skt. *karuna*). The heartfelt wish that all beings be free from suffering, the commitment to bring them relief, and putting that aspiration into practice by serving all.

cyclical existence. *See* samsara.

daka (Skt.; Tib. khadro, *mkha' 'gro*, "sky-goer"). A class of buddhas and accomplished beings in male form.

dakini (Skt.; Tib. khadroma, *mkha' 'gro ma*, "sky-goer"). A term used in esoteric teachings, with several meanings: (1) A buddha in female form. (2) The emptiness principle of the union of wisdom and emptiness, or wisdom of wisdom and skillful means, or emptiness of emptiness and compassion. (3) A highly accomplished female spirit-being who protects and guides the esoteric teachings and their followers. Dakinis can be in peaceful, wrathful, or semiwrathful form.

development and perfection stages. The two stages in tantric meditation. The development stage refers to visualizations of the Buddha mandala. The perfection stage refers to the attainment of realizations and accomplishments of power and wisdom.

Dharmakaya (Skt.; Tib. chöku, *chos sku*). One of the three aspects of a Buddha; the ultimate body that is pure and emptiness. *See also* three bodies.

dual obscurations. Emotional obscurations and intellectual obscurations, which obstruct us from realizing our true nature.

dualistic concepts. Thinking based on a discriminating mentality that constantly emphasizes opposites, dividing experience into subject and object, "self" and "other." In contrast, the enlightened mind sees all simultaneously and nondually, as oneness without limit. Dualistic concepts arise as soon as our mind grasps at the "self" of any mental object, perceiving mental objects as truly existing entities. Note that all dualistic concepts and emotions—even positive ones—are accompanied by grasping at "self." So although positive emotions are good, they still fall short of perfection, which is the primordial wisdom beyond dualistic thinking and emotional sensations. Grasping at positive qualities is nonetheless a stepping-stone to perfection, helping us eventually to loosen the grasping at "self" and to experience sensations of peace and joy. So transforming from negative to positive, and then from positive to perfection, is the way to move toward the full perfection of Buddhahood.

Dzogpa Chenpo (Tib. *rdzogs pa ch'en po*; Skt. Mahasandhi or Atiyoga). Also called Dzogchen (*rdzogs ch'en*). The highest

level of the nine vehicles (*yanas*) or stages of view, meditation, and attainment, according to the Nyingma school of
Tibetan Buddhism.

eight consciousnesses. The consiousnesses of the eye, ear, nose,
tongue, body, mind (Skt. *manovijnana*), defiled mind (Skt.
klishtamanas, "klesha-mind"), and universal ground (Skt.
alayavijnana).

Eightfold Noble Path. Right understanding, right thought, right
speech, right action, right livelihood, right effort, right
mindfulness, and right concentration. According to the
Fourth Noble Truth, this is the path of freedom as taught
by the Buddha.

emanation. *See* tulku.

emptiness (Skt. *shunyata;* Tib. tongpa nyid, *stong pa nyid*). This
term in Buddhist philosophy may be better translated as
"openness," which denotes the unrestricted, uncontrived,
unbounded, unhindered, nondual, unchanging, and fully
awakened state, Buddhahood. *See also* openness.

Emptiness in Mahayana is the highest view to be realized. It means total freedom from the conceptually fabri-
cated fetters that we create to bind ourselves. New students
sometimes confuse "emptiness" with "nothingness" or the
absence of anything, but that is a nihilistic notion that does
not convey or lead to the qualities of *shunyata*.

If we understand the meaning of emptiness, we free
ourselves from our chains of concepts and emotions, and
awaken from the nightmare of samsara. Such realization
and freedom can be attained through forceful meditations
such as the unconditional devotion and unconditional loving-kindness discussed in this book. It is also possible to
realize emptiness through reasoning—by realizing that
everything appears merely through interdependent causes
and conditions, like illusions without any true existence.

When we experience this realization, all our tightness,

stress, confusion, and pain will dissipate. We will fully awaken from the illusory nightmare-like struggle of life. That is the realization of the true wisdom of emptiness, absolute freedom—Buddhahood.

So emptiness is wisdom and wisdom is emptiness. For example, the most important training to attain the sixth perfection—wisdom (Tib. *sherab*; Skt. *prajna*)—is meditation on emptiness.

engaged bodhichitta (Tib. jugpa semkye, '*jug pa sems bskyed*). Also called "putting bodhichitta into practice." The second stage of developing bodhichitta. We develop it by putting into practice the aspirations that we developed earlier (at the stage of aspirational bodhichitta), such as by serving others, praying, contemplating, and realizing the true emptiness nature. *See also* aspirational bodhichitta.

enlightened mind. The true nature of the mind; the awakened state, Buddhahood.

enlightenment (Tib. sang-gye, *sangs rgyas*; Skt. *buddha*). The goal and result of Buddhist trainings; the awakening of Buddhahood. *See also* Buddhahood.

esoteric Buddhism. Vajrayana (the "Diamond Vehicle"), one of the major schools of Mahayana Buddhism. Vajrayana follows the esoteric teachings of Tantra. Its trainings focus on pure perception: seeing, hearing, and feeling everything as Buddha-forms, Buddha-sounds, and Buddha-wisdom. Its goal is to attain the three Buddha-bodies (*kayas*), Buddhahood, for the sake of all mother-beings. *See also* Tantra.

exoteric Buddhism. *See* Sutra.

five paths. The fivefold path of Mahayana training. (1) The path of accumulation (Tib. tsoglam, *tshogs lam*; Skt. *sambhara-marga*), (2) the path of joining/application (Tib. jorlam, *sbyor lam*; Skt. *prajoya-marga*), (3) the path of insight (Tib. thonglam, *mthong lam*; Skt. *darshana-marga*), (4) the path of meditation (Tib. gomlam, *bsgom lam*; Skt. *bhavana-marga*), and (5) the path of no-more-training (Tib. miloplam, *mi slob lam*; Skt. *ashaiksha-marga*).

Five Perfections. The first five of the Six Perfections: generosity, discipline, patience, diligence, and contemplation. Progressing in these five will help the practitioner to reach the sixth perfection, wisdom.

five wisdoms of Buddhahood. (1) Ultimate wisdom (Tib. chöying yeshe, *ch'os dbying ye shes*; Skt. *dharmadhatu-jnana*); (2) mirror-like wisdom (Tib. melong, *me long ye shes*; Skt. *adarsha-jnana*); (3) wisdom of equality (Tib. nyam-nyi, *mnyam nyid ye shes*; Skt. *shamata-jnana*); (4) discriminative (or discerning; all-knowing) wisdom (Tib. sortog, *sor rtog ye shes*; Skt. *pratyavekshana-jnana*); and all-accomplishing wisdom (Tib. jadrup, *bya grub ye shes,* Skt. *krityanushthana-jnana*). *See also* wisdom.

fivefold wisdoms. *See* five wisdoms of Buddhahood.

four boundless attitudes (Tib. tsemepa zhi, *tshad med pa bzhi*; Skt. *chaturaprameya*; "four immeasurables"). The following four attitudes are each accompanied by the wish that beings become enlightened: (1) loving-kindness (Tib. jampa, *byams pa*; Skt. *maitri*), (2) compassion (Tib. nyingje, *snying rje*; Skt. *karuna*), (3) sympathetic joy (Tib. gawa, *dga' ba*; Skt. *mudita*), and (4) equanimity (Tib. tang-nyom, *btang snyoms*; Skt. *upeksha*). *See also* four virtuous attitudes.

four causes of taking rebirth in the pure land. (1) Thinking about the details of the Pure Land, (2) making merits, (3) developing bodhichitta, the aspiration "May all take rebirth in the Pure Land," and (4) dedicating all the merits that you have to all beings, as the seed for them to take rebirth in the Pure Land, and making aspiration prayers for this.

four virtuous attitudes (Tib. tsangpe nepa zhi, *tshangs pa'i gnas pa bzhi*; Skt. *brahmavihara*, "divine attitude"). Thoughts of (1) loving-kindness (wishing joy to all beings), (2) compassion (wishing that all beings should be free from suffering), (3) sympathetic joy (rejoicing in the happiness of others), and (4) equanimity (wishing well toward all beings equally). In this training, one does not wish for both beings' happiness and their full enlightenment; compare the entry for "four boundless attitudes."

fourfold enlightened bodies. The four bodies (Skt. *kayas*) of Buddhahood: (1) ultimate essence: emptiness, the primordial purity (Tib. ngowo nyi ku, *ngo bo nyid sku*; Skt. *svabhavikakaya*); (2) ultimate body (Tib. chökyi ku, *chos kyi sku*; Skt. *dharmakaya*); (3) enjoyment body (Tib. longchö dzog ku, *longs spyod rdzogs sku*; Skt. *sambhogakaya*); (4) emanated body (Tib. trulpe ku, *sprul pa'i sku*; Skt. *nirmanakaya*). *See also* three bodies.

grasping at "self" (Tib. dagdzin, *bdag 'dzin*; Skt. *atmagriha*). Getting attached to or becoming possessive about any mental object, in ourselves or others. When we see a mental object as if it were a truly existing entity, we are grasping at it. As our minds tighten the grip of this grasping, we suffer. Thus, grasping at "self" is the root of afflicting emotions. *See also* dualistic concepts.

Hayagriva (Skt.; Tib. Tamdrim, *rta mgrin*). A wrathful form of Avalokiteshvara. He is usually depicted as red, with a horse's head protruding from his head.

interdependent arising (Tib. tendrel, *rten 'brel*; Skt. *pratityasamutpada*). Also translated as interdependent causation, dependent origination, dependent coarising, and codependent origination. According to Buddhism, mental states and physical phenomena do not develop or function independently, by chance, or by virtue of some higher power, but rather through the interdependence of causes and conditions. When we realize the ultimate nature and attain enlightenment, we relinquish our ignorance and in so doing we stop the wheel of the "twelve links of interdependent arising": ignorance (unenlightened state), formation, consciousness, name and form, the six sense faculties, contact, feeling, craving, clinging, becoming, birth, and old age and death.

karma (Skt.). The natural law of causation. A habitual pattern sown in our mind stream by our thoughts, words, and deeds. Our karmic patterns determine the kind of life experiences we will have, now and in the future. The word also sometimes means simply a deed or action.

Kuan Yin (Chinese, Guanyin; Japanese, Kannon). The bodhisattva or Buddha of Compassion or Loving-Kindness, in female form.

loving-kindness (Tib. jampa, *byams pa;* Skt. *maitri;* Pali, *metta*). The thought of wishing joy for all beings, or the vow of bringing joy to all. A related term, *bodhichitta,* is the vow to bring Buddhahood to all. In this book, we are meditating on loving-kindness *and* the development of bodhichitta together—taking the vow of bringing both happiness and enlightenment to all beings.

loving-kindness free from concepts (Tib. migpa mepe jampa, *dmigs pa med pa'i byams pa*). Unconditional love purified of concepts, emotions, and sensations. The highest stage of loving-kindness training, which is the perfection of loving-kindness and compassion.

Madhyamaka (Skt.; Tib. wuma, *dbu ma*). The Middle Way, a Mahayana philosophical school founded by Nagarjuna. Following the Middle Way entails not adhering to extreme views, such as eternalism and nihilism.

Mahamudra (Skt., "Great Seal"). Meditation practices of the highest sutric and tantric teachings.

Mahayana (Skt.). The Great Vehicle. One of the three major divisions of Buddhism, and the type practiced in Tibetan Buddhism. In the Mahayana, the trainings that lead to enlightenment are called the ten stages and five paths.

mala (Skt.). Rosary or prayer beads used in mantra practice or recitation.

mandala (Skt.; Tib. kyil khor, *dkyil 'khor*). (1) An assembly of many deities. (2) A circle of deities. (3) An altar for esoteric rites. (4) A symbol or diagram of the Buddha Pure Land.

manifested pure land. *See* pure land.

mantra (Skt.; Tib. ngak, *sngags*). Sacred syllables, sounds, and expressions with esoteric meaning and power as taught in Tantra. Mantras are used as extraordinary prayers to invoke the Buddhas, expressions of mystical energies, and manifestations of esoteric power itself. *See also* OM MA-NI PAD-ME HUNG.

mara (Skt.). A demonic or evil figure.

meditative absorption (Skt. *dhyana*). There are four main meditative absorptions (Tib. samten zhi, *bsam gtan bzhi*; Skt. *chatvari dhyanasamapatti*). In the first absorption, you focus your mind pointedly and settle with both concepts and discernment (Tib. *rtog pa* and *dpyod pa*); in the second absorption with delight (Tib. *dga' ba*); in the third absorption with bliss (Tib. *bde ba*); and in the fourth with equanimity (Tib. *btang snyoms*).

merit (Tib. sönam, *bsod nams*; Skt *punya*). The positive effect of practicing virtuous thoughts and deeds. Accumulating merits (Tib. tsog sag, *tshogs bsags*) involves skillful means such as practicing virtuous thoughts, generosity, moral discipline, tolerance, diligence, patience, and contemplation. It also includes devotion, prayers, and loving-kindness with concepts. Merit making is one of the two accumulations. *See* two accumulations.

mindstream. The continuous flow of moments of consciousness.

mother-beings. All sentient beings. Every being, even the smallest insect, has in one lifetime or another been our mother. We are therefore taught to regard all mother-beings with loving compassion.

nectar of light. Blessing nectar whose true nature is wisdom-light. Nectar of lights is inseparable from the Buddha and his Pure

Land since all are wisdom-light in their true nature. *See also* wisdom-light.

Nirmanakaya (Skt.; Tib. tulku, *sprul sku*) *See* three bodies; tulku.

nirvana (Skt.; Tib. nyangen le depa, *mya ngan las 'das pa*). The cessation of sorrow and cyclic existence, samsara. Through spiritual training we attain the cessation of ignorance and afflicting emotions and experience everlasting peace and joy. In Mahayana teachings, however, nirvana is not the fully enlightened state of Buddhahood, which transcends both the suffering of samsara and the mere peace of nirvana.

nondual. Free from objective and subjective duality.

obscurations, two (Tib. dribnyi, *sgrib gnyis*; Skt, *divi-avarana*). Emotional obscurations (Tib. nyöndrib, *nyon sgrib*; Skt. *kleshavarana*) and intellectual obscurations (obscurations of dualistic concepts, Tib. shedrib, *shes sgrib*; Skt. *jnanavarana*).

OM MA-NI PAD-ME HUNG. The mantra of the Buddha of Loving-Kindness, the most popular mantra in Tibetan Buddhism, sometimes referred to as the Six-Syllable Mantra (or Prayer). The last syllable, HUM, is pronounced by Tibetans as HUNG (*hoong*). People from Central Tibet often pronounce PADME as *peme*. *See also* Six-Syllable Mantra.

openness. In this book, "openness" mostly refers to emptiness (Skt. *shunyata*; Tib. tongpa nyi, *stong pa nyid*). The word "openness" might convey the meaning of *tongpa nyi* better for many readers than its common, literal translation, "emptiness." However, I sometimes use "openness" to convey the feeling of an open heart. So not all the instances of "openness" in this book are the technical translation of *tongpa nyi*. When citing lines of texts, however, I tried to stick with the literal term, "emptiness." *See also* emptiness.

perfection stages. *See* development and perfection stages.

pure land (Tib. zhingkham, *zhing khams*; Skt. *buddhakshetra*, "Buddha-field"). A world or paradise of everlasting peace and joy, an abode of the Buddhas and enlightened ones.

The absolute pure land is the state of Dharmakaya and Sambhogakaya, the true Buddhahood and Buddha Pure Land that can be perceived only by the enlightened ones. Then there are infinite Nirmanakaya pure lands, worlds of peace and joy, manifested by the Buddhas in various forms so that fortunate beings can enjoy them. After taking rebirth in a Nirmanakaya Pure Land, the attainment of Buddhahood will be certain. *See also* Blissful Pure Land.

refuge. Going for refuge means taking protection in or guidance of the Buddha, Dharma, and Sangha.

relative truth. *See* two truths.

Sambhogakaya (Skt.; Tib. long-ku, *longs sku*). *See* three bodies.

samsara (Skt.; Tib. khorba, *'khor ba*). The six realms of cyclic existence, in which beings endlessly live, die, and take rebirth in higher and lower realms, depending on their karma. *Samsara* is a synonym for our mundane world.

sending and receiving. *See* tonglen.

Sevenfold Vairochana Posture. (1) Sit with crossed legs (also known as lotus posture); (2) rest hands in the lap, right palm on top of left palm, facing up; (3) spine held up straight; (4) shoulders spread; (5) head and chin are slightly lowered; 6) tip of the tongue touching the upper palate; and (7) eyes gazing past the tip of the nose. The important thing in all postures is sitting straight. When your spine is straight, the channels, arteries, and veins will be straight. When these are straight, the breathing will be balanced. When the breathing is normal, mind functions more calmly and clearly.

Shakyamuni Buddha. The historical Buddha of this world age, whose epithet means "Sage of the Shakya clan." He lived around the fifth century B.C.E.

Six Perfections (Skt. *paramita*, "perfection"). The path of the bodhisattva includes training in and perfecting six virtues: generosity (or giving), discipline (or moral conduct), patience, diligence, contemplation, and wisdom. The first five perfections are the accumulation of merits. The sixth perfection is the accumulation of wisdom.

Six-Syllable Prayer. The prayer or mantra of Avalokiteshvara, the Buddha of Loving-Kindness: OM MA-NI PAD-ME HUM. The last syllable is pronounced HUNG (*hoong*) by Tibetans. In the *terma* tradition, the heart-seed syllable of Avalokiteshvara (HRI) is added at the end, making it a prayer of seven syllables. The Six Syllables are referred to as a prayer in the common teachings of Buddhism. In tantric chanting practice, it is called a mantra.

skillful means (Tib. tab, *thabs;* Skt. *upaya*). One of the two major ways of training in Buddhism; the other is wisdom (Tib. sherab, *shes rab;* Skt. *prajna*). Skillful means are all the positive concepts and activities of relative truth, such as generosity, moral discipline, patience, diligence, contemplation, compassion, and effort. Wisdom consists of meditative training, realization of absolute truth, and freedom from concepts. The combination of both wisdom and skillful means leads us to enlightenment.

suchness (Skt. *tathata;* Tib. dezhinnyi, *de bzhin nyid*). The true nature, as it is.

Sutra. The tradition of exoteric Buddhist teachings; the common path. The sutras are the Buddha's oral teachings that were later written down by his disciples.

Tantra. The tradition of esoteric Buddhist teachings, known as the uncommon path (in contrast to the common path, which is Sutra). Many of the tantras, or tantric texts, are believed to have been taught by the historical Buddha and other Buddhas. *See also* esoteric Buddhism.

ten stages. The stages (Skt. *bhumis*) that a bodhisattva passes through on the path to becoming a Buddha.

ten virtuous deeds. Refraining from the ten unvirtuous deeds: (1) three unvirtuous deeds of the mind—greed, anger, and ignorance; (2) four unvirtuous deeds of speech—telling lies, divisive speech, harsh words, and gossip; and (3) three unvirtuous deeds of the body—killing, stealing, and sexual misconduct.

ter (Tib. *gter,* "treasured ones"). Also called *terma* (*gter ma*). Mystically concealed and discovered Dharma treasures. Guru Padmasambhava concealed many esoteric teachings and religious objects around the eighth century C.E. for the benefit of future humanity. From the eleventh century through today, the rebirths of his disciples have been rediscovering these *ter* through their mystical power. *Ter* teachings are practiced mainly by the Nyingma school of Tibetan Buddhism. For details of the *ter* tradition, see *Hidden Teachings of Tibet* by Tulku Thondup.

tertön (Tib. *gter ston*). One who discovers *ter.*

Theravada (Pali, "way of the elders"). A branch of Dharma that originated in one of the early schools of Buddhism and that now flourishes in Southeast Asia. It is considered one of the three main divisions of Buddhism, the others being Mahayana and Vajrayana.

three bodies (Skt. *trikaya;* Tib. kusum, *sku gsum*). The three aspects of Buddhahood. The ultimate body (Skt. *dharmakaya*) is the pure emptiness aspect of Buddhahood. The enjoyment body (Skt. *sambhogakaya*) is the true Buddha-form body as enjoyed by Buddhas. They possess the richness of Buddha-qualities and the prosperity of the Buddha pure lands, but all in an everlasting state of oneness. The manifested body (Skt. *nirmanakaya*) is the physical form in which ordinary beings see the forms of a Buddha. Mahayana texts adds a fourth, transcendent body. *See also* fourfold enlightened bodies.

three disciplines (Tib. dompa, *sdom pa*). The discipline of individual liberation (the path of Theravada monks and nuns), bodhisattva discipline (the Mahayana), and tantric discipline (the Vajrayana).

three doors. Body (Skt. *kaya*; Tib. lu, *lus*), speech (Skt. *vak*; Tib. ngak, *nyag*), and mind (Skt. *chitta*; Tib. yi, *yid*).

three poisons. Three primary unvirtuous emotions or mental states: greed, hatred, and ignorance.

three worlds. Also called the three existents: the desire world, the form world, and the formless world. The desire realm is our world. The world of form is the realm of lesser celestial beings, and the formless world is the realm of higher celestial beings.

tonglen (Tib. *gtong len*). Sending and receiving (or giving and taking), a meditation practice in which you give your happiness to others and take others' suffering upon yourself through the power of compassion and loving-kindness.

tulku (Tib. *sprul sku*; Skt. *nirmanakaya*). *Emanation, manifestation* and *incarnation* are different words for the Tibetan term *tulku*—one of the three bodies or aspects of Buddhahood. According to Buddhism, ordinary beings take rebirth, whether as humans, animals, or other beings, propelled by their karma, their past positive and negative mental and physical deeds. Highly accomplished adepts, however, do not need to take rebirth because they have transcended concepts and emotions, the root of karma. Instead, they emanate whatever forms would be helpful to others. The Buddhas could emanate infinite manifestations, as they are not limited by karmic conditions, but act out of boundless loving-kindness. See *Incarnation* by Tulku Thondup.

twelve links of interdependent arising. *See* interdependent arising.

two accumulations (Tib. tsoknyi, *tshogs gnyis*). Creating merits and realizing high stages of wisdom. Both are needed to attain Buddhahood. Accumulating merits (Tib. sonam, *bsod nams*; Skt, *punya*) involves skillful means such as practicing virtuous thoughts, generosity, moral discipline, tolerance, diligence, patience, and contemplation. It also includes devotion, prayers, and loving-kindness with concepts. Accumulating wisdom (Tib. sherab, *shes rab;* Skt. *prajna*) involves realizing the true nature of all, emptiness, as it is.

two truths. (1) The absolute (or ultimate) truth of the Dharma, and (2) the relative (or conventional) truth of the world of appearances. Absolute truth is the true nature of all phenomenal existence, loving-kindness free from concepts, and emptiness. Relative truth is phenomenal existence that arises through interdependent causation. It is what ordinary beings see and feel, all the dualistic virtuous and unvirtuous deeds, concepts, and sensual feelings.

vajra posture. *See* Sevenfold Vairochana Posture.

Vajrayana (Skt., "diamond vehicle"). *See* esoteric Buddhism.

wisdom. Used to translate two Tibetan words, *sherab* and *yeshe,* with different meanings. (1) *Sherab* (Tib. *shes rab;* Skt. *prajna*) refers to knowledge, wisdom, or realization, starting from the ordinary knowledge of accurately understanding the meaning of a text, all the way to the highest realization of the wisdom of Buddhahood. The sixth perfection (paramita) refers to wisdom (sherab) in this latter sense. (2) *Yeshe* (Tib. *ye shes;* Skt. *jnana*) refers exclusively to the highest wisdom of Buddhahood. It is the omniscient wisdom, free from concepts, encompassing the five wisdoms of Buddhahood and, in this book, the essence of the Fourth Buddha Stage. *See also* five wisdoms of Buddhahood; two accumulations.

wisdom of equality (Tib. nyam-nyi yeshe, *mnyam nyid ye shes;* Skt. *samata-jnana*). One of the five wisdoms of Buddhahood; the perfection of loving-kindness and compassion.

wisdom-light. Also known as "the natural light of wisdom" or "the radiance of wisdom." In the relative sense, the pure light and nectar emanating from the Buddha's body and wisdom. In the absolute sense, Buddha wisdom and Buddha wisdom-light are in union. Lights are the spontaneously appearing luminosity of the Buddha's wisdom itself. That is, we are the light and the light is us: all are one.

wisdom-light body. At death, very highly accomplished meditators could dissolve their gross body into a mass of light. Then that light will also dissolve. That is a sign that they have purified, not only their mind, but also their gross body, into ultimate purity—the body of wisdom-light, Buddhahood.

BIBLIOGRAPHY

Tibetan Works Cited

Tibetan titles in this list are given in a modified Wylie transliteration, arranged according to the abbreviations used in the endnotes.

BGD *Byams pa sgom pa'i mdo.* Sherab Natshog. Vol. Ka. Kajur. Dege Edition.

BLC *Byang ch'ub lam rim ch'e ba,* by Je Tsongkhapa. Published by the Corporate Body of the Buddha Educational Foundation, Taiwan.

BMB *lo gros mi zad pas bstan pa'i mdo.* Dode. Vol. Ma. Kajur. Dege Edition.

BNB *la rnam la nye bar mkho ba'i yi ge,* by the Third Dodrupchen. Jigme Tenpei Nyima'i Sungbum. Vol. Ja. Golok Edition, China.

BP   *Byang ch'ub sems dpa'i spyod pa la'jug pa* (Skt. *Bodhisattvacharyavatara,* Way of the Bodhisattva), by Shantideva. Dodrupchen Monastery Edition, China.

BTT *dBu ma rtsa bai tshigs le-ur byas pa shes rab,* by Nagarjuna. Published by the Corporate Body of the Buddha Educational Foundation, Taiwan, 1990.

CCL *Ch'os bchu pa'i leu.* Kontseg. Vol. Kha. Kajur. Dege Edition.

CRN   *Bya bral ch'os dbyings rang grol gyi rnam thar dang gsung skor.* Published by Serta Dzong, China, 1992.

CSN   *bChom ldan 'das ma shes rab kyi pha rol tu phyin pa'i snying po.* Shes rab sna tshogs. Vol. Ka. Kajur. Dege Edition.

CT   *Ch'ed du brjod pa'i tshoms.* Dode. Vol. Sa. Kajur. Dege Edition.

CYD   *'Phags pa ch'os yang dag par sdud pa zhes bya ba theg pa ch'en po'i mdo.* Dode. Vol. Zha. Kajur. Dege Edition.

DDN   *mDo sde dran pa nye bar bzhag pa.* Dode. Vol. Ra. Kajur. Dege Edition.

DDRS   *bsTod tshogs,* by the Third Dodrupchen. Jigme Tenpe'i Nyima'i Sungbum. Vol. 1. Sichuan Mirig Petrunkhang, China.

DGT   *De bzhin gshegs pa brgyad la bstod pa,* by Shantarakshita. Totsog. Vol. Ka. Tenjur. Dege Edition. Reproduced by Mirig Petrunkhang, China.

DMZ   *Dri ma med par grags pas zhus pa'i mdo.* Dode. Vol. Ma. Kajur. Dege Edition.

DNC   *Don rnam par nges pa zhes bya ba'i ch'os kyi rnam grangs.* Dode. Vol. Sa. Kajur. Dege Edition.

DNN   *sDom gsum rnam par nges pa,* by Padma Wangi Gyalpo. Published by Khamtul Rinpoche, Kalimpong, India.

DPK   *Dam pa'i ch'os padma dkar po* (Skt., *Saddharmapundarika*). Dode. Vol. Ja. Kajur. Dege Edition.

DTD   *mDo ting 'dzin rgyal po.* Dode. Vol. Da. Kajur. Dege Edition.

DTG   *Man ngag rdo rje'i thol glu spros bral sgra dbyangs.* Patrul Nyentsom Chedu. Sichuan Mirig Petrunkhang, China.

DT   *SmDzod tik thar lam gsal byed,* by Gyalwa Gedundrub. Tibetan Monastery, Sarnath, Varanasi, India, 1973.

GB   *rGyud bla ma'i bstan bchos,* by Maitreya-natha. Gyu Lame'i Tenchö Tsadrel. Sichuan Mirig Petrunkhang, China.

GCT   *Yon tan rin po ch'e'i mdzo kyi bsdus 'grel rgya mtsho'i* ch'u thigs, by the First Dodrupchen. Yönten Dzö Tsadrel. Sichuan Mirig Petrunkhang, China.

GPK   rGyab ch'os padma dkar po, by Ju Mipham Rinpoche. Mipham Sungbum. Vol. Ch'a. Dege Edition.

GR   'Phags pa rgya ch'er rol pa. Dode. Vol. Kha. Kajur. Dege Edition.

GRT   sGom rim tha ma, by Kamalashila. Wuma. Vol. Ki. Tenjur. Dege Edition. W23703.

GSG   mNgon pa mdzod kyi mch'an 'grel dbyig gnyen dgongs pa gsal ba'i sgron me, by Losal Wangpo. Ngonpa Dzo Tsadrel. Sichuan Mirig Petrunkhang, China, 1996.

GSL   rGyal ba'i sras kyi lag len sum chu so bdun ma, by Tsunpa Thogme. Gyalse Laglen Tsadrel. Sichuan Mirig Petrunkhang, China.

GT   brGyad stong pa. Sher phyin. Vol. Ka. Kajur. Dege Edition.

JZK   'Jam dpal zhing gi yon tan bkod pa. Kontseg. Vol. Ga. Kajur. Dege Edition.

KBZ   Kun bzang bla ma'i zhal lung, by Patrul Rinpoche. Sichuan Edition, China.

KDL   sKyid sdug lam 'khyer, by the Third Dodrupchen. Jigme Tenpe'i Nyima'i Sungbum. Vol. Ja. Golok Edition, China.

KSG   'Phags pa thugs rje ch'en po'i khrid gzhung gsal ba'i sgron me. Discovered by Rigdzin Godem. Thugje Chenpo Droba Kungrol Gyi Tsapö. Vol. 1. Block print. TBRC W27296.

KT   dKon mch'og ta la la'i mdo. Dode. Vol. Pa. Kajur. Dege Edition.

KTS   dKon brtsegs. Vol. Kha. Kajur. Dege Edition.

KZBZ   sNying thig sngon 'gro kun bzang bla ma'i zhal lung gi zin bris, by Pema Ledreltsal. Sichuan Mirig Petrunkhang, China.

LS   'Phags pa lang-kar gshegs pa'i mdo [Skt. Lankavatara Sutra] sangs rgyas thams chad kyi gsung gi snying po. Dode. Vol. Cha. Kajur. Dege Edition.

MKB   Mani bka' 'bum, by Chogyal Srongtsen Gampo. Vol. E. Puthang Dewachen Edition, Bhutan. TBRC W19225.

MNG   *mNgon par rtogs pa'i rgyan*, by Maitreya-natha. Taiwan Edition.

NKT   *mNgon pa kun las btus pa*, by Asanga. Ngonpa. Vol. Ri. Tenjur. Dege Edition. TBRC W23703.

OKD   *'Phags pa od dpag med kyi bkod pa zhes bya ba theg pa ch'en po'i mdo*. Kontseg. Vol. Ka. Kajur. Dege Edition.

PHC   *Sangs rgyas phal bo ch'e zhes bya ba shin tu rgyas pa ch'en po'i mdo*. Phalbo Che. Vol. Ah. Kajur. Dege Edition.

PT   *dPa' bar 'gro ba'i ting nge 'dzin*. Dode. Vol. Da. Kajur. Dege Edition.

RCZ   *Ri ch'os mtshams kyi zhal gdams*, by Karma Chagme. Published by Tashijong, India.

RP   *Rin po ch'e'i phreng ba*, by Nagarjuna. Wuma Rigtsog Drug. Taiwan Edition.

RZD   *Nang sgrub rig 'dzin 'dus pa'i zin bris Rig 'dzin zhal lung bde ch'en dpal ster,* by Chechog Dondruptsal. Golok Edition, China.

SDT   *gSang ba rnal 'byor ch'en po'i rgyud rdo rje rtse mo*. Gyudbum. Vol. Nya. Dege Edition.

SLD   *gSol 'debs le-u bdun ma*. Discovered by Rigdzin Godem. Dudjom Chöchö. Kalimpong Edition, India.

SMC   *gSol 'debs smon lam phyogs bsdus*. Jigme Tenpe'i Nyima'i Sungbum. Vol. Ka. Golok Edition, China.

SNS   *ems nyid ngal gso*, by Longchen Rabjam. Adzom Edition.

SNR   *Sems nyid ngal gso'i rang 'grel,* by Longchen Rabjam. Adzom Edition.

SR   *rDzogs pa ch'en po sems nyid rang grol*, by Longchen Rabjam. Adzom Edition.

ST   *gSung thor bu*, by Je Tsongkhapa. Je'i Sungbum. Vol. Kha. Lhasa Edition.

STC   *'Phags pa shes rab kyi pha rol tu phyin pa tshigs su bchad pa*. Sherab Natshog. Vol. Ka. Kajur. Dege Edition.

STG   *Sher phyin stong phrag brgya pa*. Sher phyin. Vol. Ka. Kajur. Dege Edition.

TBN   *rTen ching 'brel bar 'byung ba dang po dang rnam par dbye ba bstan pa zhes bya ba'i mdo.* Dode. Vol. Tsha. Dege Edition.

TBS   *rTen 'brel gyi bshad pa,* by Lushul Khenpo Konchog Dronme. Dodrupchen Khenchen Namzhi Sungchö Chogdrig. Vol. Om. Sanglung Gon, Dzika, China.

TBT   *Thub ch'og byin rlabs gter mdzod,* by Mipham Rinpoche. Mipham Sungbum. Vol. Ch'a. Dege Edition.

TG   *Thar pa rin po ch'e'i rgyan,* by Je Sönam Rinchen (Gampopa). Sichuan Edition, China.

TGR   *Thub pa'i dgongs pa rab tu gsal ba,* by Sakya Pandita. Photoprint.

TTB   *Thog mtha' bar gsum du dge ba'i gtam,* by Patrul Rinpoche. Patrul Nyentsom Chedu. Sichuan, China.

TY   *Thugs ch'en yig drug gi skor tsho,* by the Third Dodrupchen. Dodrupchen Sungbum. Vol. Nga. Golok Penying Edition, Sichuan, China.

TYN   *Thugs rje ch'en po'i mngon rtogs yid bzhin nor bu.* Discovered by Rigdzin Godem. Thugje Chenpo Droba Kungrol. Tsapod. Vol. 1. TBRC W27296.

TZG   *Tshad med bzhi'i rgya ch'er 'grel ba,* by Buddhagupta. Wuma. Vol. Ki. Tenjur. Dege Edition. TBRC W23703-110.

YD   *Yon tan rin po ch'e'i mdzod dga' ba'i ch'ar* (Treasury of Precious Qualities), by Jigme Lingpa. Yönten Dzo Tsadrel. Sichuan Mirig Petrunkhang, China.

YNG   *Lam rim ye shes snying po'i 'grel pa ye shes snang ba rab tu rgyas pa,* by Lodrö Thaye. Rinchen Terdzö. Vol. 96. Ngodrup and Sherab Drimay, Paro, Bhutan, 1976–1980. TBRC W20578.

YRD   *Yid bzhin rin po che'i mdzod,* by Longchen Rabjam. Vol. E. Adzom Edition.

ZGD   *Zhing mch'og bgrod pa'i bde lam,* by the Third Dodrupchen. Jigme Tenpe'i Nyima'i Sungbum. Vol. Ch'a. Golok Edition, China.

ZLB   *gZhi lam 'bras bu'i smon lam,* by Jigme Lingpa. Nyingthig
      Doncha. Choten Gonpa Edition. India

ZPD   *Zhal gdams phyogs bsdus,* by the Third Dodrupchen.
      Jigme Tenpe'i Nyima'i Sungbum. Vol. Ka. Golok Edition,
      China.

ZTR   *Zhi khro dgongs pa rang grol gyi las byang ch'ung ba tshor ba
      rang grol (Zhitro Gongpa Rangtrol),* discovered by Karma
      Lingpa. Zhitro Gongpa Rangtrol. Vol. Om. Sherab
      Drime, Sikkim, India.

English-Language Books by Tulku Thondup

*Boundless Healing: Meditation Exercises to Enlighten the Mind and
      Heal the Body.* Boston: Shambhala Publications, 2000.

Buddhist Civilization in Tibet. New York: Routledge & Kegan
      Paul, 1987.

*The Dzogchen: Innermost Essence Preliminary Practice (Long-chen
      Nying-thig Ngon-dro),* by Jig-me Lingpa. Translated with
      commentary by Tulku Thondup. 2nd rev. ed. New Delhi:
      Paljor Publications, 1987.

Enlightened Journey: Buddhist Practice as Daily Life. Boston: Sham-
      bhala Publications, 1995.

Enlightened Living: Teachings of Tibetan Buddhist Masters. Kath-
      mandu: Rangjung Yeshe Publications, 1997.

*The Healing Power of Loving-Kindness: A Guided Buddhist Medita-
      tion.* Boston: Shambhala Publications, 2009.

*The Healing Power of Mind: Simple Meditation Exercises for Health,
      Well-Being, and Enlightenment.* Boston: Shambhala Publica-
      tions, 1998.

*Hidden Teachings of Tibet: An Explanation of the Terma Tradition
      of Tibetan Buddhism.* Boston: Wisdom Publications, 1986.

*Incarnation: The History and Mysticism of the Tulku Tradition of Ti-
      bet.* Boston: Shambhala Publications, 2011.

Masters of Meditation and Miracles: The Longchen Nyingthig Lin-

eage of Tibetan Buddhism. Boston: Shambhala Publications, 1996.

Peaceful Death, Joyful Rebirth: A Tibetan Buddhist Guidebook. Boston: Shambhala Publications, 2005.

The Practice of Dzogchen: Longchen Rabjam's Writings on the Great Perfection. Rev. and exp. ed. Introduced, translated, and annotated by Tulku Thondup. Edited by Harold Talbott. Boston: Snow Lion, 2014.

Other English-Language References

Blofeld, John. Bodhisattva of Compassion: The Mystical Tradition of Kuan Yin (1977). Boston: Shambhala Publications, 2009.

Goleman, Daniel. Destructive Emotions: A Scientific Dialogue with the Dalai Lama. New York: Bantam Books, 2004.

Suzuki, D. T. Buddha of Infinite Light. Boston: Shambhala Publications, 1997.

INDEX

confidence
in developing devotion and
trust, 44, 49–50, 76
examples of, 147–50
lack of, 72, 74
in loving-kindness of Buddha, 65
in positive objects and
qualities, 31–32
in Ultimate Buddha Stage,
83
confusion, dealing with, 45–46
contemplation, 46, 85, 93
contentment, 145
crown lord, 95, 205
cyclic existence. *See* samsara

dakas, 121–22, 232
dakinis, 122, 217n4, 232–33
death
of accomplished medita-
tors, 194
of others, practices for,
197–98
power of positive thoughts
and deeds at, 148–49
rebirth and, 193–94
wisdom-light body at, 246
dedications, 157–58, 206–8,
213
Deer Park, 23
deities, unity of, 98–99
Destructive Emotions (Goleman), 22

development and perfection
stages, 204, 233
devotees, examples of, 146–50
devotion, 41
to all Enlightened Ones, 99
benefits of, 6, 47, 144–45
conceptual, 134
confidence in, 76
dedication and, 157, 158
developing, 42–43
energy of, 100–101
for healing, 167, 168, 171,
172–73
as life goal, 126
meditation on, 3
merit of, 85–86
in non-Buddhist traditions,
150
to ordinary objects, exercising caution in, 139
in Outer Buddha Stage,
71, 73
positive training of, 31
praying with, 101–3
radiating Buddha's love
through, 2
rekindling, 116
results of, 48–52, 102
in seeing true nature, 85
self-reinforcing quality
of, 45
in Six-Syllable Mantra/
Prayer, 34, 104
dharani, 117, 224n130

Index · 260

four boundless attitudes,
60–62, 236
traditional aspiration
prayer of, 62, 202–3,
222n84
Four Buddha Stages, 156
aspiration for, 11–12
benefits of, 51
combined with tonglen,
191–92
dedication and aspiration
in, 157–58
esoteric meditation prac-
tice, correspondences to,
201, 204
inspiration for, 4
interdependent arising and,
26–27
progression, importance of,
141–42, 145
short practice, 209–13
summary of, 5–6
See also Inner Buddha
Stage; Outer Buddha
Stage; Universal Buddha
Stage; Ultimate Buddha
Stage
four causes of taking rebirth in
the Pure Land, 195-96
Four Noble Truths, 22–24
four virtuous attitudes, 61, 134,
236–37
fourfold enlightened bodies,
237

Fourth Dodrupchen Rin-
poche, 12, 217n1

Gampopa Sönam Rinchen,
225n146
on loving-kindness, 65,
66–67
Garab Dorje, 225nn148–49
gardening with Six Perfections, 184–85
Gelug school, 69–70
Goleman, Daniel, 22
Golok, Eastern Tibet, 146
grasping
confusion and, 45–46
cutting at root, 155–56
expiration of, 130–31
at loving-kindness, 74
at meditative experiences,
76
at ordinary things, 47
positive, 145–46
at positive objects, 30
at positive qualities, 30, 145,
146, 233
as root of pain, 172
at thoughts and sensations,
83
triple cycle of, 134
See also self
Great Wisdom Mother (Prajnaparamita), 131, 132
Guru Rinpoche. See Padma-
sambhava

habitual patterns, 238
  of neutrality, 153–56
  reflected at death, 149
  transforming, 180–81
  See also mental habits
happiness
  contaminated and un-
    contaminated, 69–70,
    222n103
  and enlightenment, dis-
    tinctions in wish for,
    59–62, 68
  loving-kindness toward
    others as cause, 54
  transforming into spiritual
    path, 161, 176–78
  universal desire for, 58–59
  from virtuous attitude,
    59–60
Hayagriva, 96, 237
healing, 167, 178
  by lights, 38, 117, 168–69
  by nectar of light, 170–71
  of others, 116, 172
  through purification and
    blessings, 110
Healing Buddha, 117
human nature, 53

ignorance, 24–26, 154
illness. *See* sickness
imagination, 83
individual liberation, 134
indivisibility, 84, 94

Inner Buddha Stage, 11, 124
  practice instructions,
    113–19
  short practice of, 211–12
  view of, 71–72, 78, 113
inspiration, 42–43
intention, setting, 90, 210
interdependent arising, 24–27,
  237–38

Jigme Lingpa, 220n48
  on loving-kindness causing
    attachment, 188
  on result, 133
  on Three Jewels, 44
Jigme Tenpe Nyima. *See* Third
  Dodrupchen
Jigme Thrinle Ozer. *See* First
  Dodrupchen Rinpoche
Jowo (also Jowoje Atisha). *See*
  Atisha
joy
  from Buddha lights, 126
  dedication and, 158
  from devotion and trust,
    44–45, 48
  of loving-kindness, 53
  wishing for others, 188

Kadam school, 225n144
Kagyu school, 66–67, 224n128
Kamalashila, 226n162
  on discernment, 155–56
karma, 76–77, 238

merit (*continued*)
    rebirth and, 194, 195–96
    trust in, 31
    while facing difficulties, 160
mind
    appearance and, 79
    Buddhist training of, 152
    Buddhist view of, 172
    at death, 149, 193–94
    deluded, 17–18, 23
    grasping of, 40
    guarding from wrong
        thoughts, 189–90
    influence of thoughts on,
        185–86
    as light, 113–14
    merging with Buddha's, 110
    ordinary and enlightened
        aspects of, 17–20
    protecting, 138–39
    purifying, 173
    transforming, 1, 20–22,
        47–48, 71–72, 77, 78, 79,
        121
    trust in, 32
    unity of Buddha's with
        ours, 52
    in Universal Buddha Stage,
        122, 123, 124
    visualization, effects on,
        91, 92
Mind of the Great Beings
    (bodhichitta), 48
mindfulness, 138–39, 189–90

Mind-Only (Yogachara)
    school, 218n9
mindstream, definition of, 239
Mipham Rinpoche
    on meditating on lights, 117
    on personal deities, 98–99
mirror-like wisdom, 105, 161,
    236
moon cushion, visualization
    of, 92
mother-beings, 74, 239
    aspiration for rebirth of,
        197–98
    dedications to, 158, 206–8
    extending loving-kindness
        toward, 118, 119
    kindness of, 67, 68
    recognizing all beings as,
        58–59, 63
    wishing happiness and en-
        lightenment for, 61–62

Nagarjuna, 222n95
    on benefits of loving-kind-
        ness, 162
    on bodies of Buddhas, 164
    on causes of rebirth, 142–43
    on expiration of grasping,
        131
    on two truths, 150–51
    on wishing joy for infinite
        beings, 65
natural radiance, 79, 134
    See also self-radiation

nectar of light, 37, 168–69,
170–71, 239–40
negative actions, 74–75, 229
See also unvirtuous deeds
negative emotions, 229
antidotes to, 179–81
from attachment to mundane objects, 47
effect on rebirth, 142–43,
193
purifying, 160–61, 210
subsiding of, 55
tonglen and, 192
See also afflicting emotions
Ngulchu Thogme, 225n144
on evil friends, 186
on guarding mind from
negativity, 190
Nirmanakaya, 231, 237, 241,
243–44
See also three bodies
nirvana, 49, 61, 240
nonduality, 8, 80, 133–34, 240
nonreturners, 117, 224n131
no-self, 132–33, 225n151
See also self
Nyingma school, 68–69,
221n57, 225n149, 234, 243

obscurations, 85, 164
See also dual obscurations
obstacles, 74–76, 176–78
OM MA-NI PAD-ME HUNG, definition of, 240

See also Six-Syllable Mantra/
Prayer
omniscient wisdom, 94–95, 97,
128, 132
See also wisdom; wisdom-
mind, of Buddha
openness, 234–35, 240
resting in, 175–76
in Ultimate Buddha Stage,
84–85, 127–28
See also emptiness
ornamental costumes, thirteen, 94, 223n115
Outer Buddha Stage, 11, 204
benefits of, 145, 151–52
in developing devotion,
43, 51
four tools in, 32
keeping connection with, 73
preparation and intention,
89–90
short practice of, 210–11
view of, 71
visualization, 91–96

Padma Karpo, Yidzhin Dzod-
grel, 156
Padma Wangchen, Pandita,
221n74
on benefiting all, 59
Padmasambhava, 98, 99, 204,
218–19n20, 240–41, 243
on developing trust, 43
on importance of trust, 31

merit of, 85–86

as positive words and sounds, 30

power in transforming mind, 21–22

refuge, 202

See also Six-Syllable Mantra/Prayer

precious human life, 126, 154

preliminary practices, 135, 201–2

projections, 18–19, 172

Pure Land tradition, 44

pure lands, 241

Adorned by a Thousand Worlds, 160

blessing lights from, 37, 38–40

Blissful Pure Land, 144, 194–98, 230, 231

rebirth in, 148, 194–96, 236

Tushita Heaven, 218n9

visions of at death, 148–49

visualization of, 121–24

pure perception, 6, 40, 47, 139, 235

purification, 109–11, 116–17, 118, 192

purity, 53–54, 65, 92, 95, 223n113, 237, 246

reasoning, 234–35

rebirth, 244–45

causes of, 40, 193–94

effect of thought patterns on, 154–55

in higher realms, 144

from negative emotions and unvirtuous deeds, 142–43

from virtuous attitude, 59–60

See also pure lands, rebirth in

refuge, 42, 99, 201–2, 215, 241

rejoicing, 72, 74, 80, 137, 158

relative truth, 245.

See also two truths

Rigdzin Godem, 201, 204, 219n21, 223n109

on indivisibility, 84

on union of appearance and emptiness, 81–82

sadhana, 204–6

Sage of Great Accomplishments, 12, 217n1

See also Fourth Dodrupchen Rinpoche

Sakya school, 67–68

Samantabhadra, 207, 228n206

Sambhogakaya, 94, 232

See also three bodies

samsara, 12, 241

cause of, 40

contemplating faults of, 42, 44

Four Noble Truths and, 23–24

Uttara Tantra, 32

vajra posture, 94, 241
Vajrayana, 134, 219, 235, 241
    See also esoteric Buddhism
Victorious Ones, 64, 222n91
Vinaya, 226–27n179, 232
virtue, 41, 48, 59–60, 61, 130
virtuous attitude, 59
    See also four virtuous atti-
        tudes
visualization
    devotion and, 101–2
    for emotional healing,
        172–74
    in esoteric meditation prac-
        tice, 203, 204–6
    for physical healing, 168–71
    positive objects in, 29–30
    of pure lands, 121–22
    purpose of, 91
    reasons for, 77–78
    of sky, flower, moon cush-
        ion, 91–92
    See also Buddha of
        Loving-Kindness
        (Avalokiteshvara)

wisdom
    accumulation of, 85–86
    denial of, 155
    discernment as root of, 155
    emptiness and, 235

as key Buddha quality,
    32–34
meanings of, 245–46
nondual, 134
perfection of, 144, 150–51,
    184
radiance of, 39
skillful means and, 85–86
symbols of, 104
twofold, 105, 130
    See also five wisdoms of
        Buddhahood; omni-
        scient wisdom; sixth
        perfection
wisdom of equality, 9, 105, 236,
    246
wisdom-light body, 20, 246
wisdom-lights, 239–40, 246
    absolute and relative mean-
        ing of, 39–40
    of Buddha's body, 93–94
    inherent quality of mind,
        195
    of nondual wisdom, 134
    perception of, 80
    of Pure Land, 38
wisdom-mind, of Buddha, 37,
    97, 124–25
Wish-fulfilling Gem, The:
    The Liturgy of the Bud-
    dha of Loving-Kindness,
    204–5
wish-fulfilling gems, 64, 94